Hard Press

Isaac Bickerstaff, Physician and Astrologer
by Richard Steele.
Papers from Steele's "Tatler."

Introduction by Henry Morley.

Of the relations between Steele and Addison, and the origin of Steele's "Tatler," which was developed afterwards into the "Spectator," account has already been given in the introduction to a volume of this Library, * containing essays from the "Spectator"— "Sir Roger de Coverley and the Spectator Club." There had been a centre of life in the "Tatler," designed, as Sir Roger and his friends were designed, to carry the human interest of a distinct personality through the whole series of papers. The "Tatler's" personality was Isaac Bickerstaff, Physician and Astrologer; as to years, just over the grand climacteric, sixty-three, mystical multiple of nine and seven; dispensing counsel from his lodgings at Shire Lane, and seeking occasional rest in the vacuity of thought proper to his club at the "Trumpet."

The name of Isaac Bickerstaff Steele borrowed from his friend Swift, who, just before the establishment of the "Tatler," had borrowed it from a shoemaker's shop-board, and used it as the name of an imagined astrologer, who should be an astrologer indeed, and should attack John Partridge, the chief of the astrological almanack makers, with a definite prediction of the day and hour of his death. This he did in a pamphlet that brought up to the war against one stronghold of superstition an effective battery of satire. The pamphlet itself has been given in our volume of "The Battle of the Books, and other short pieces, by Jonathan Swift." * The joke once set rolling was kept up in other playful little pamphlets written to announce the fulfilment of the prophecy, and to explain to Partridge that, whether he knew it or not, he was dead. This joke was running through the town when Steele began his "Tatler" on the 12th of April, 1709. Steele kept it going, and, in doing so, wrote once or twice in the character of Bickerstaff. Then he proceeded to develop the astrologer into a central character, who should give life and unity to his whole series of essays.

They were published for a penny a number, at the rate of three numbers a week. Steele, for his threepence a week, sought to give wholesome pleasure while good-humouredly helping men to rise above the vices and the follies of their time. Evil ways of the court of Charles the Second still survived in empty tradition. The young man thought it polite to set up for an atheist, said Steele, though it could be proved on him that every night he said his prayers. It was fashionable to speak frivolously of women, and affect contempt of marriage, though the English were, and are, of all men the most domestic. Steele made it a part of his duty to break this evil custom, to uphold the true honour of womanhood, and assert the sacredness of home. The two papers in this collection, called "Happy Marriage" and "A Wife Dead," are beautiful examples of his work in this direction. He attacked the false notions of honour that kept duelling in fashion. Steele could put his heart into the direct telling of a tale of human love or sorrow, and in that respect was unapproached by Addison; but he was surpassed by Addison in a subtle delicacy of touch, in the fine humour with which he played about the whims and weaknesses of men. The tenth paper in this volume, "A Business Meeting," is a good example of what Addison could do in that way.

Of the papers in this volume, the first was sent to Steele by the post, and—Steele wrote in the original Preface to the completed "Tatler"—"written, as I since understand, by Mr. Twisdon, who died at the battle of Mons, and has a monument in Westminster Abbey, suitable to the respect which is due to his wit and valour." The other papers were all written by Steele, with these exceptions:—No. V., "Marriage of Sister Jenny," and No. VII., "The Dream of Fame," were described by Steele, in a list given to Tickell, as written by himself and Addison together. No. XIV., "The Wife Dead," is Steele's, with some passages to which Addison contributed. No. XIII., "Dead Folks," was, the first part, by Addison; the second part, beginning "From my own Apartment, November 25," by Steele; Addison wrote No. X., "A Business Meeting," No. XVI., "A very Pretty Poet," and No. XX., "False Doctoring." Addison joined Steele in the record of cases before "Bickerstaff, Censor," No. XVIII. Of the twenty-six sections in this volume, therefore, three are by Addison alone; one is in two parts, written severally by Addison and Steele; four are by Addison and Steele working in friendly fellowship, and without trace of their separate shares in the work; eighteen are by Steele alone.

* Cassell's National Library.

ISAAC BICKERSTAFF, PHYSICIAN AND ASTROLOGER.

I.—THE STAFFIAN RACE.

From my own Apartment, May, 4, 1709.

Of all the vanities under the sun, I confess that of being proud of one's birth is the greatest. At the same time, since in this unreasonable age, by the force of prevailing custom, things in which men have no hand are imputed to them; and that I am used by some people as if Isaac Bickerstaff, though I write myself Esquire, was nobody: to set the world right in that particular, I shall give you my genealogy, as a kinsman of ours has sent it me from the Heralds' Office. It is certain, and observed by the wisest writers, that there are women who are not nicely chaste, and men not severely honest, in all families; therefore let those who may be apt to raise aspersions upon ours please to give us as impartial an account of their own, and we shall be satisfied. The business of heralds is a matter of so great nicety that, to avoid mistakes, I shall give you my cousin's letter, verbatim, without altering a syllable.

"Dear cousin,
"Since you have been pleased to make yourself so famous of late by your ingenious writings, and some time ago by your learned predictions; since Partridge, of immortal memory, is dead and gone, who, poetical as he was, could not understand his own poetry; and, philomathical as he was, could not read his own destiny; since the Pope, the King of France, and great part of his court, are either literally or metaphorically defunct: since, I say, these things not foretold by any one but yourself have come to pass after so surprising a manner: it is with no small concern I see the original of the Staffian race so little known in the world as it is at this time; for which reason, as you have employed your studies in astronomy and the occult sciences, so I, my mother being a Welsh woman, dedicated mine to genealogy, particularly that of our family, which, for its antiquity and number, may challenge any in Great Britain. The Staffs are originally of Staffordshire, which took its name from them; the first that I find of the Staffs was one Jacobstaff, a famous and renowned astronomer, who, by Dorothy his wife, had issue seven sons—viz., Bickerstaff, Longstaff, Wagstaff, Quarterstaff, Whitestaff, Falstaff, and Tipstaff. He also had a younger brother, who was twice married, and had five sons—viz., Distaff, Pikestaff, Mopstaff, Broomstaff, and Raggedstaff. As for the branch from whence you spring, I shall say very little of it, only that it is the chief of the Staffs, and called Bickerstaff, quasi Biggerstaff; as much as to say, the Great Staff, or Staff of Staffs; and that it has applied itself to Astronomy with great success, after the example of our aforesaid forefather. The descendants from Longstaff, the second son, were a rakish, disorderly sort of people, and rambled from one place to another, till, in the time of Harry the Second, they settled in Kent, and were called Long-Tails, from the long tails which were sent them as a punishment for the murder of Thomas-a-Becket, as the legends say. They have been always sought after by the ladies, but whether it be to show their aversion to popery, or their love to miracles, I cannot say. The Wagstaffs are a merry, thoughtless sort of people, who have always been opinionated of their own wit; they have turned themselves mostly to poetry. This is the most

6

numerous branch of our family, and the poorest. The Quarterstaffs are most of them prize-fighters or deer-stealers; there have been so many of them hanged lately that there are very few of that branch of our family left. The Whitestaffs are all courtiers, and have had very considerable places. There have been some of them of that strength and dexterity that five hundred of the ablest men in the kingdom have often tugged in vain to pull a staff out of their hands. The Falstaffs are strangely given to drinking: there are abundance of them in and about London. And one thing is very remarkable of this branch, and that is, there are just as many women as men in it. There was a wicked stick of wood of this name in Harry the Fourth's time, one Sir John Falstaff. As for Tipstaff, the youngest son, he was an honest fellow; but his sons, and his sons' sons, have all of them been the veriest rogues living; it is this unlucky branch has stocked the nation with that swarm of lawyers, attorneys, serjeants, and bailiffs, with which the nation is overrun. Tipstaff, being a seventh son, used to cure the king's evil; but his rascally descendants are so far from having that healing quality that, by a touch upon the shoulder, they give a man such an ill habit of body that he can never come abroad afterwards. This is all I know of the line of Jacobstaff; his younger brother, Isaacstaff, as I told you before, had five sons, and was married twice; his first wife was a Staff, for they did not stand upon false heraldry in those days, by whom he had one son, who, in process of time, being a schoolmaster and well read in the Greek, called himself Distaff or Twicestaff. He was not very rich, so he put his children out to trades, and the Distaffs have ever since been employed in the woollen and linen manufactures, except myself, who am a genealogist. Pikestaff, the eldest son by the second venter, was a man of business, a downright plodding fellow, and withal so plain, that he became a proverb. Most of this family are at present in the army. Raggedstaff was an unlucky boy, and used to tear his clothes in getting birds' nests, and was always playing with a tame bear his father kept. Mopstaff fell in love with one of his father's maids, and used to help her to clean the house. Broomstaff was a chimney-sweeper. The Mopstaffs and Broomstaffs are naturally as civil people as ever went out of doors; but, alas! if they once get into ill hands, they knock down all before them. Pilgrimstaff ran away from his friends, and went strolling about the country; and Pipestaff was a wine-cooper. These two were the unlawful issue of Longstaff.

"N.B.—The Canes, the Clubs, the Cudgels, the Wands, the Devil upon two Sticks, and one Bread, that goes by the name of Staff of Life, are none of our relations. I am, dear Cousin,
      "Your humble servant,
          "D. *Distaff*.

"From the Heralds' Office,
      "May 1, 1709."

II.—PACOLET.

From my own Apartment, May 8.

Much hurry and business have to-day perplexed me into a mood too thoughtful for going into company; for which reason, instead of the tavern, I went into Lincoln's Inn walks; and having taken a round or two, I sat down, according to the allowed familiarity of these places, on a bench; at the other end of which sat a venerable gentleman, who, speaking with a very affable air, "Mr. Bickerstaff," said he, "I take it for a very great piece of good fortune that you have found me out." "Sir," said I, "I had never, that I know of, the honour of seeing you before." "That," replied he, "is what I have often lamented; but, I assure you, I have for many years done you good offices, without being observed by you; or else, when you had any little glimpse of my being concerned in an affair, you have fled from me, and shunned me like an enemy; but, however, the part I am to act in the world is such that I am to go on in doing good, though I meet with never so many repulses, even from those I oblige." This, thought I, shows a great good nature, but little judgment, in the persons upon whom he confers his favours. He immediately took notice to me that he observed, by my countenance, I thought him indiscreet in his beneficence, and proceeded to tell me his quality in the following manner: "I know thee, Isaac, to be so well versed in the occult sciences that I need not much preface, or make long preparations, to gain your faith that there are airy beings who are employed in the care and attendance of men, as nurses are to infants, till they come to an age in which they can act of themselves. These beings are usually called amongst men guardian angels; and, Mr. Bickerstaff, I am to acquaint you that I am to be yours for some time to come; it being our orders to vary our stations, and sometimes to have one patient under our protection, and sometimes another, with a power of assuming what shape we please, to ensnare our wards into their own good. I have of late been upon such hard duty, and know you have so much work for me, that I think fit to appear to you face to face, to desire you will give me as little occasion for vigilance as you can." "Sir," said I, "it will be a great instruction to me in my behaviour if you please to give me some account of your late employments, and what hardships or satisfactions you have had in them, that I may govern myself accordingly." He answered, "To give you an example of the drudgery we go through, I will entertain you only with my three last stations. I was on the first of April last put to mortify a great beauty, with whom I was a week; from her I went to a common swearer, and have been last with a gamester. When I first came to my lady, I found my great work was to guard well her eyes and ears; but her flatterers were so numerous, and the house, after the modern way, so full of looking-glasses, that I seldom had her safe but in her sleep. Whenever we went abroad, we were surrounded by an army of enemies; when a well-made man appeared, he was sure to have a side-glance of observation; if a disagreeable fellow, he had a full face, out of more inclination to conquests; but at the close of the evening, on the sixth of the last month, my ward was sitting on a couch, reading Ovid's epistles; and as she came to this line of Helen to Paris,

'She half consents who silently denies,'

8

entered Philander, who is the most skilful of all men in an address to women. He is arrived at the perfection of that art which gains them; which is, 'to talk like a very miserable man, but look like a very happy one.' I saw Dictinna blush at his entrance, which gave me the alarm; but he immediately said something so agreeable on her being at study, and the novelty of finding a lady employed in so grave a manner, that he on a sudden became very familiarly a man of no consequence, and in an instant laid all her suspicions of his skill asleep, as he had almost done mine, till I observed him very dangerously turn his discourse upon the elegance of her dress, and her judgment in the choice of that very pretty mourning. Having had women before under my care, I trembled at the apprehension of a man of sense who could talk upon trifles, and resolved to stick to my post with all the circumspection imaginable. In short, I prepossessed her against all he could say to the advantage of her dress and person; but he turned again the discourse, where I found I had no power over her, on the abusing her friends and acquaintance. He allowed, indeed, that Flora had a little beauty, and a great deal of wit; but then she was so ungainly in her behaviour, and such a laughing hoyden! Pastorella had with him the allowance of being blameless; but what was that towards being praiseworthy? To be only innocent is not to be virtuous! He afterwards spoke so much against Mrs. Dipple's forehead, Mrs. Prim's mouth, Mrs. Dentifrice's teeth, and Mrs. Fidget's cheeks that she grew downright in love with him; for it is always to be understood that a lady takes all you detract from the rest of her sex to be a gift to her. In a word, things went so far that I was dismissed. The next, as I said, I went to was a common swearer. Never was a creature so puzzled as myself when I came first to view his brain; half of it was worn out, and filled up with mere expletives that had nothing to do with any other parts of the texture; therefore, when he called for his clothes in a morning, he would cry, 'John!' John does not answer. 'What a plague! nobody there? What the devil, and rot me, John, for a lazy dog as you are!' I knew no way to cure him but by writing down all he said one morning as he was dressing, and laying it before him on the toilet when he came to pick his teeth. The last recital I gave him of what he said for half an hour before was, 'What, the devil! where is the washball? call the chairmen! d—n them, I warrant they are at the alehouse already! zounds! and confound them!' When he came to the glass he takes up my note—'Ha! this fellow is worse than me: what, does he swear with pen and ink?' But, reading on, he found them to be his own words. The stratagem had so good an effect upon him that he grew immediately a new man, and is learning to speak without an oath; which makes him extremely short in his phrases; for, as I observed before, a common swearer has a brain without any idea on the swearing side; therefore my ward has yet mighty little to say, and is forced to substitute some other vehicle of nonsense to supply the defect of his usual expletives. When I left him, he made use of 'Odsbodikins! Oh me! and Never stir alive!' and so forth; which gave me hopes of his recovery. So I went to the next I told you of, the gamester. When we first take our place about a man, the receptacles of the pericranium are immediately searched. In his I found no one ordinary trace of thinking; but strong passion, violent desires, and a continued series of different changes had torn it to pieces. There appeared no middle condition; the triumph of a prince, or the misery of a beggar, were his alternate states. I was with him no longer than one day, which was yesterday. In the morning at twelve we were worth four thousand pounds; at three, we were arrived at six thousand; half an hour after, we were reduced to one thousand; at four of the clock, we were down to two hundred; at

9

five, to fifty; at six, to five; at seven, to one guinea; the next bet to nothing. This morning he borrowed half a crown of the maid who cleans his shoes, and is now gaming in Lincoln's Inn Fields among the boys for farthings and oranges, till he has made up three pieces, and then he returns to White's into the best company in town."

Thus ended our first discourse; and it is hoped that you will forgive me that I have picked so little out of my companion at our first interview. In the next it is possible he may tell me more pleasing incidents; for though he is a familiar, he is not an evil, spirit.

III.—PACOLET'S STORY.

From my own Apartment, May 12.

I have taken a resolution hereafter, on any want of intelligence, to carry my Familiar abroad with me, who has promised to give me very proper and just notices of persons and things, to make up the history of the passing day. He is wonderfully skilful in the knowledge of men and manners, which has made me more than ordinarily curious to know how he came to that perfection, and I communicated to him that doubt. "Mr. Pacolet," said I, "I am mightily surprised to see you so good a judge of our nature and circumstances, since you are a mere spirit, and have no knowledge of the bodily part of us." He answered, smiling, "You are mistaken; I have been one of you, and lived a month amongst you, which gives me an exact sense of your condition. You are to know that all who enter into human life have a certain date or stamen given to their being which they only who die of age may be said to have arrived at; but it is ordered sometimes by fate, that such as die infants are, after death, to attend mankind to the end of that stamen of being in themselves which was broken off by sickness or any other disaster. These are proper guardians to men, as being sensible of the infirmity of their State. You are philosopher enough to know that the difference of men's understandings proceeds only from the various dispositions of their organs; so that he who dies at a month old is in the next life as knowing, though more innocent, as they who live to fifty; and after death they have as perfect a memory and judgment of all that passed in their lifetime as I have of all the revolutions in that uneasy, turbulent condition of yours; and you would say I had enough of it in a month were I to tell you all my misfortunes." "A life of a month cannot have, one would think, much variety. But pray," said I, "let us have your story."

Then he proceeds in the following manner:—

"It was one of the most wealthy families in Great Britain into which I was born, and it was a very great happiness to me that it so happened, otherwise I had still, in all probability, been living; but I shall recount to you all the occurrences of my short and miserable existence, just as, by examining into the traces made in my brain, they appeared to me at that time. The first thing that ever struck my senses was a noise over my head of one shrieking; after which, methought, I took a full jump, and found myself in the hands of a sorceress, who seemed as if she had been long waking and employed in some incantation: I was thoroughly frightened, and cried out; but she immediately seemed to go on in some magical operation, and anointed me from head to foot. What they meant I could not imagine; for there gathered a great crowd about me, crying, 'An heir! an heir!' upon which I grew a little still, and believed this was a ceremony to be used only to great persons, and such as made them, what they called Heirs. I lay very quiet; but the witch, for no manner of reason or provocation in the world, takes me, and binds my head as hard as possibly she could; then ties up both my legs, and makes me swallow down a horrid mixture. I thought it a harsh entrance into life, to begin with taking physic; but I was forced to it, or else must have taken down a great instrument in which she gave it me. When I was thus

11

dressed, I was carried to a bedside, where a fine young lady, my mother I wot, had like to have hugged me to death. From her they faced me about, and there was a thing with quite another look from the rest of the room, to whom they talked about my nose. He seemed wonderfully pleased to see me; but I knew since, my nose belonged to another family. That into which I was born is one of the most numerous amongst you; therefore crowds of relations came every day to congratulate my arrival; among others my cousin Betty, the greatest romp in nature; she whisks me such a height over her head that I cried out for fear of falling. She pinched me, and called me squealing chit, and threw me into a girl's arms that was taken in to tend me. The girl was very proud of the womanly employment of a nurse, and took upon her to strip and dress me a-new, because I made a noise, to see what ailed me; she did so, and stuck a pin in every joint about me. I still cried; upon which she lays me on my face in her lap; and, to quiet me, fell a-nailing in all the pins by clapping me on the back and screaming a lullaby. But my pain made me exalt my voice above hers, which brought up the nurse, the witch I first saw, and my grandmother. The girl is turned downstairs, and I stripped again, as well to find what ailed me as to satisfy my grandam's farther curiosity. This good old woman's visit was the cause of all my troubles. You are to understand that I was hitherto bred by hand, and anybody that stood next gave me pap, if I did but open my lips; insomuch that I was grown so cunning as to pretend myself asleep when I was not, to prevent my being crammed. But my grandmother began a loud lecture upon the idleness of the wives of this age, who, for fear of their shape, forbear suckling their own offspring; and ten nurses were immediately sent for; one was whispered to have a wanton eye, and would soon spoil her milk; another was in a consumption; the third had an ill voice, and would frighten me instead of lulling me to sleep. Such exceptions were made against all but one country milch-wench, to whom I was committed, and put to the breast. This careless jade was eternally romping with the footman and downright starved me; insomuch that I daily pined away, and should never have been relieved had it not been that, on the thirtieth day of my life, a Fellow of the Royal Society, who had writ upon Cold Baths, came to visit me, and solemnly protested I was utterly lost for want of that method; upon which he soused me head and ears into a pail of water, where I had the good fortune to be drowned; and so escaped being lashed into a linguist till sixteen, and being married to an ill-natured wife till sixty, which had certainly been my fate had not the enchantment between body and soul been broken by this philosopher. Thus, till the age I should have otherwise lived, I am obliged to watch the steps of men; and, if you please, shall accompany you in your present walk, and get you intelligence from the aerial lackey, who is in waiting, what are the thoughts and purposes of any whom you inquire for."

I accepted his kind offer, and immediately took him with me in a hack to White's.

- - - - -

White's Chocolate-house, May 13.

12

We got in hither, and my companion threw a powder round us, that made me as invisible as himself; so that we could see and hear all others, ourselves unseen and unheard.

The first thing we took notice of was a nobleman of a goodly and frank aspect, with his generous birth and temper visible in it, playing at cards with a creature of a black and horrid countenance, wherein were plainly delineated the arts of his mind, cozenage, and falsehood. They were marking their game with counters, on which we could see inscriptions, imperceptible to any but us. My Lord had scored with pieces of ivory, on which were writ, "Good Fame, Glory, Riches, Honour, and Posterity!" The spectre over-against him had on his counters the inscriptions of "Dishonour, Impudence, Poverty, Ignorance, and Want of Shame." "Bless me!", said I; "sure, my Lord does not see what he plays for?" "As well as I do," says Pacolet. "He despises that fellow he plays with, and scorns himself for making him his companion." At the very instant he was speaking, I saw the fellow who played with my Lord hide two cards in the roll of his stocking. Pacolet immediately stole them from thence; upon which the nobleman soon after won the game. The little triumph he appeared in, when he got such a trifling stock of ready money, though he had ventured so great sums with indifference, increased my admiration. But Pacolet began to talk to me. "Mr. Isaac, this to you looks wonderful, but not at all to us higher beings: that nobleman has as many good qualities as any man of his order, and seems to have no faults but what, as I may say, are excrescences from virtues. He is generous to a prodigality, more affable than is consistent with his quality, and courageous to a rashness. Yet, after all this, the source of his whole conduct is, though he would hate himself if he knew it, mere avarice. The ready cash laid before the gamester's counters makes him venture, as you see, and lay distinction against infamy, abundance against want; in a word, all that is desirable against all that is to be avoided." "However," said I, "be sure you disappoint the sharpers to-night, and steal from them all the cards they hide." Pacolet obeyed me, and my Lord went home with their whole bank in his pocket.

IV.—RECOLLECTIONS.

It is remarkable that I was bred by hand, and ate nothing but milk till I was a twelvemonth old; from which time, to the eighth year of my age, I was observed to delight in pudding and potatoes; and, indeed, I retain a benevolence for that sort of food to this day. I do not remember that I distinguished myself in anything at those years but by my great skill at taw, for which I was so barbarously used that it has ever since given me an aversion to gaming. In my twelfth year, I suffered very much for two or three false concords. At fifteen I was sent to the university, and stayed there for some time; but a drum passing by, being a lover of music, I listed myself for a soldier. As years came on, I began to examine things, and grew discontented at the times. This made me quit the sword, and take to the study of the occult sciences, in which I was so wrapped up that Oliver Cromwell had been buried, and taken up again, five years before I heard he was dead. This gave me first the reputation of a conjurer, which has been of great disadvantage to me ever since, and kept me out of all public employments. The greater part of my later years has been divided between Dick's coffee-house, the Trumpet in Sheer Lane, and my own lodgings.

- - - - -

From my own Apartment, June 5.

There are those among mankind who can enjoy no relish of their being except the world is made acquainted with all that relates to them, and think everything lost that passes unobserved; but others find a solid delight in stealing by the crowd, and modelling their life after such a manner as is as much above the approbation as the practice of the vulgar. Life being too short to give instances great enough of true friendship or good-will, some sages have thought it pious to preserve a certain reverence for the Manes of their deceased friends; and have withdrawn themselves from the rest of the world at certain seasons, to commemorate in their own thoughts such of their acquaintance who have gone before them out of this life. And indeed, when we are advanced in years, there is not a more pleasing entertainment than to recollect in a gloomy moment the many we have parted with that have been dear and agreeable to us, and to cast a melancholy thought or two after those with whom, perhaps, we have indulged ourselves in whole nights of mirth and jollity. With such inclinations in my heart I went to my closet yesterday in the evening, and resolved to be sorrowful; upon which occasion I could not but look with disdain upon myself, that though all the reasons which I had to lament the loss of many of my friends are now as forcible as at the moment of their departure, yet did not my heart swell with the same sorrow which I felt at that time; but I could, without tears, reflect upon many pleasing adventures I have had with some, who have long been blended with common earth. Though it is by the benefit of nature that length of time thus blots out the violence of afflictions; yet with tempers too much given to pleasure, it is almost necessary to revive the old places of grief in our memory; and ponder step by step on past life, to lead the mind into that sobriety of thought which poises the heart, and makes it beat with due time, without being quickened with desire, or retarded with despair, from its proper and equal motion. When we wind up a clock that is out of order, to make it go well for the future, we do not immediately set the hand to the present instant, but we make it strike the round of all its hours, before it can recover the regularity of its time. Such, thought I, shall be my method this evening; and since it is that day of the year which I dedicate to the memory of such in another life as I much delighted in when living, an hour or two shall be sacred to sorrow and their memory, while I run over all the melancholy circumstances of this kind which have occurred to me in my whole life.

The first sense of sorrow I ever knew was upon the death of my father, at which time I was not quite five years of age; but was rather amazed at what all the house meant than possessed with a real understanding why nobody was willing to play with me. I remember I went into the room where his body lay, and my mother sat weeping alone by it. I had my battledore in my band, and fell a-beating the coffin, and calling Papa; for, I know not how, I had some slight idea that he was locked up there. My mother catched me in her arms, and, transported beyond all patience of the silent grief she was before in, she almost smothered me in her embrace; and told me in a flood of tears, "Papa could not hear me, and would play with me no more, for they were going to put him under ground, whence he could never come to us again." She was a very beautiful woman, of a noble spirit, and there was a dignity in her grief amidst all the wildness of her transport which, methought, struck me with an instinct of sorrow, which, before I was sensible of what it was to grieve, seized my very soul, and has made pity the weakness of my heart ever since. The mind in infancy is, methinks, like the body in embryo; and receives impressions so forcible that they are as hard to be removed by reason as any mark with which a child is born is to be taken away by any future application. Hence it is that good-nature in me is no merit; but having been so frequently overwhelmed with her tears before I knew the cause of any affliction, or could draw defences from my own judgment, I imbibed commiseration, remorse, and an unmanly gentleness of mind, which has since ensnared me into ten thousand calamities; and from whence I can reap no advantage, except it be that, in such a humour as I am now in, I can the better indulge myself in the softness of humanity, and enjoy that sweet anxiety which arises from the memory of past afflictions.

We, that are very old, are better able to remember things which befell us in our distant youth than the passages of later days. For this reason it is that the companions of my strong and vigorous years present themselves more immediately to me in this office of sorrow. Untimely or unhappy deaths are what we are most apt to lament: so little are we able to make it indifferent when a thing happens, though we know it must happen. Thus we groan under life, and bewail those who are relieved from it. Every object that returns to our imagination raises different passions, according to the circumstance of their departure. Who can have lived in an army, and in a serious hour reflect upon the many gay and agreeable men that might long have flourished in the arts of peace, and not join with the imprecations of the fatherless and widow on the tyrant to whose ambition they fell sacrifices? But gallant men, who are cut oft by the sword, move rather our veneration than our pity; and we gather relief enough from their own contempt of death, to make it no evil, which was approached with so much cheerfulness, and attended with so much honour. But when we turn our thoughts from the great parts of life on such occasions, and instead of lamenting those who stood ready to give death to those from whom they had the fortune to receive it; I say, when we let our thoughts wander from such noble objects, and consider the havoc which is made among the tender and the innocent, pity enters with an unmixed softness, and possesses all our souls at once.

Here, were there words to express such sentiments with proper tenderness, I should record the beauty, innocence, and untimely death of the first object my eyes ever beheld with love. The beauteous virgin! how ignorantly did she charm, how carelessly excel! Oh, Death! thou hast right to the bold, to the ambitious, to the high, and to the haughty; but why this cruelty to the humble, to the meek, to the undiscerning, to the thoughtless? Nor age, nor business, nor distress can erase the dear image from my imagination. In the same week, I saw her dressed for a ball, and in a shroud. How ill did the habit of death become the pretty trifler! I still behold the smiling earth—A large train of disasters were coming on to my memory, when my servant knocked at my closet-door, and interrupted me with a letter, attended with a hamper of wine, of the same sort with that which is to be put to sale on Thursday next at Garraway's coffee-house. Upon the receipt of it I sent for three of my friends. We are so intimate that we can be company in whatever state of mind we meet, and can entertain each other without expecting always to rejoice. The wine we found to be generous and warming, but with such a heat as moved us rather to be cheerful than frolicsome. It revived the spirits, without firing the blood. We commended it till two of the clock this morning; and having to-day met a little before dinner, we found that, though we drank two bottles a man, we had much more reason to recollect than forget what had passed the night before.

V.—MARRIAGE OF SISTER JENNY.

From my own Apartment, September 3O.

I am called off from public dissertations by a domestic affair of great importance, which is no less than the disposal of my sister Jenny for life. The girl is a girl of great merit and pleasing conversation: but I being born of my father's first wife, and she of his third, she converses with me rather like a daughter than a sister. I have indeed told her that if she kept her honour, and behaved herself in such a manner as became the Bickerstaffs, I would get her an agreeable man for her husband; which was a promise I made her after reading a passage in Pliny's "Epistles." That polite author had been employed to find out a consort for his friend's daughter, and gives the following character of the man he had pitched upon. "Aciliano plurimum vigoris et industriae quanquam in maxima verecundia: est illi facies liberalis, multo sanguine, multo rubore, suffusa: est ingenua totius corporis pulchritudo et quidam senatorius decor, quae ego nequaquam arbitror negligenda: debet enim hoc castitati puellarum quasi praemium dari." "Acilianus," for that was the gentleman's name, "is a man of extraordinary vigour and industry, accompanied with the greatest modesty: he has very much of the gentleman, with a lively colour, and flush of health in his aspect. His whole person is finely turned, and speaks him a man of quality; which are qualifications that, I think, ought by no means to be overlooked, and should be bestowed on a daughter as the reward of her chastity."

A woman that will give herself liberties need not put her parents to so much trouble; for if she does not possess these ornaments in a husband she can supply herself elsewhere. But this is not the case of my sister Jenny, who, I may say without vanity, is as unspotted a spinster as any in Great Britain. I shall take this occasion to recommend the conduct of our own family in this particular.

We have, in the genealogy of our house, the descriptions and pictures of our ancestors from the time of King Arthur, in whose days there was one of my own name, a knight of his round table, and known by the name of Sir Isaac Bickerstaff. He was low of stature, and of a very swarthy complexion, not unlike a Portuguese Jew. But he was more prudent than men of that height usually are, and would often communicate to his friends his design of lengthening and whitening his posterity. His eldest son Ralph, for that was his name, was for this reason married to a lady who had little else to recommend her but that she was very tall and very fair. The issue of this match, with the help of high shoes, made a tolerable figure in the next age, though the complexion of the family was obscure till the fourth generation from that marriage. From which time, till the reign of William the Conqueror, the females of our house were famous for their needlework and fine skins. In the male line there happened an unlucky accident in the reign of Richard III., the eldest son of Philip, then chief of the family, being born with a hump-back and very high nose. This was the more astonishing, because none of his forefathers ever had such a blemish, nor indeed was there any in the neighbourhood of that make, except the butler, who was noted for round shoulders and a Roman nose; what made the nose the less excusable was the remarkable smallness of his eyes.

These several defects were mended by succeeding matches: the eyes were open in the next generation, and the hump fell in a century and a half, but the greatest difficulty was how to reduce the nose, which I do not find was accomplished till about the middle of the reign of Henry VII., or rather the beginning of that of Henry VIII.

But while our ancestors were thus taken up in cultivating the eyes and nose, the face of the Bickerstaffs fell down insensibly into chin, which was not taken notice of, their thoughts being so much employed upon the more noble features, till it became almost too long to be remedied.

But length of time, and successive care in our alliances, have cured this also, and reduced our faces into that tolerable oval which we enjoy at present. I would not be tedious in this discourse, but cannot but observe that our race suffered very much about three hundred years ago, by the marriage of one of our heiresses with an eminent courtier, who gave us spindle-shanks and cramps in our bones; insomuch, that we did not recover our health and legs till Sir Walter Bickerstaff married Maud the milkmaid, of whom the then Garter King-at-Arms, a facetious person, said pleasantly enough, "that she had spoiled our blood, but mended our constitutions."

After this account of the effect our prudent choice of matches has had upon our persons and features, I cannot but observe that there are daily instances of as great changes made by marriage upon men's minds and humours. One might wear any passion out of a family by culture, as skilful gardeners blot a colour out of a tulip that hurts its beauty. One might produce an affable temper out of a shrew, by grafting the mild upon the choleric; or raise a jack-pudding from a prude, by inoculating mirth and melancholy. It is for want of care in the disposing of our children, with regard to our bodies and minds, that we go into a house and see such different complexions and humours in the same race and family. But to me it is as plain as a pikestaff, from what mixture it is that this daughter silently lours, the other steals a kind look at you, a third is exactly well behaved, a fourth a splenetic, and a fifth a coquette.

In this disposal of my sister, I have chosen with an eye to her being a wit, and provided that the bridegroom be a man of a sound and excellent judgment, who will seldom mind what she says when she begins to harangue, for Jenny's only imperfection is an admiration of her parts, which inclines her to be a little, but very little, sluttish; and you are ever to remark that we are apt to cultivate most, and bring into observation what we think most excellent in ourselves, or most capable of improvement. Thus, my sister, instead of consulting her glass and her toilet for an hour and a half after her private devotion, sits with her nose full of snuff and a man's nightcap on her head, reading plays and romances. Her wit she thinks her distinction, therefore knows nothing of the skill of dress, or making her person agreeable. It would make you laugh to see me often, with my spectacles on, lacing her stays, for she is so very a wit, that she understands no ordinary thing in the world.

18

For this reason I have disposed of her to a man of business, who will soon let her see that to be well dressed, in good humour, and cheerful in the command of her family, are the arts and sciences of female life. I could have bestowed her upon a fine gentleman, who extremely admired her wit, and would have given her a coach and six, but I found it absolutely necessary to cross the strain; for had they met, they had entirely been rivals in discourse, and in continual contention for the superiority of understanding, and brought forth critics, pedants, or pretty good poets. As it is, I expect an offspring fit for the habitation of the city, town or country; creatures that are docile and tractable in whatever we put them to.

To convince men of the necessity of taking this method, let any one even below the skill of an astrologer, behold the turn of faces he meets as soon as he passes Cheapside Conduit, and you see a deep attention and a certain unthinking sharpness in every countenance. They look attentive, but their thoughts are engaged on mean purposes. To me it is very apparent, when I see a citizen pass by, whether his head is upon woollen, silks, iron, sugar, indigo, or stocks. Now this trace of thought appears or lies hid in the race for two or three generations.

I know at this time a person of a vast estate, who is the immediate descendant of a fine gentleman, but the great grandson of a broker, in whom his ancestor is now revived. He is a very honest gentleman in his principles, but cannot for his blood talk fairly; he is heartily sorry for it; but he cheats by constitution, and over-reaches by instinct.

The happiness of the man who marries my sister will be, that he has no faults to correct in her but her own, a little bias of fancy, or particularity of manners which grew in herself, and can be amended by her. From such an untainted couple we can hope to have our family rise to its ancient splendour of face, air, countenance, manner, and shape, without discovering the product of ten nations in one house. Obadiah Greenhat says, "he never comes into any company in England, but he distinguishes the different nations of which we are composed." There is scarce such a living creature as a true Briton. We sit down, indeed, all friends, acquaintance, and neighbours; but after two bottles you see a Dane start up and swear, "the kingdom is his own." A Saxon drinks up the whole quart, and swears he will dispute that with him. A Norman tells them both, he will assert his liberty; and a Welshman cries, "They are all foreigners and intruders of yesterday," and beats them out of the room. Such accidents happen frequently among neighbours' children, and cousin-germans. For which reason I say study your race, or the soil of your family will dwindle into cits or 'squires, or run up into wits or madmen.

VI.—PROFESSIONAL: A CASE OF SPLEEN.

White's Chocolate House, October 12.

It will be allowed me that I have all along showed great respect in matters which concern the fair sex; but the inhumanity with which the author of the following letter has been used is not to be suffered:—

"Sir,
    "Yesterday I had the misfortune to drop in at my Lady Haughty's upon her visiting-day. When I entered the room where she receives company, they all stood up indeed; but they stood as if they were to stare at, rather than to receive me. After a long pause, a servant brought a round stool, on which I sat down at the lower end of the room, in the presence of no less than twelve persons, gentlemen and ladies, lolling in elbow-chairs. And, to complete my disgrace, my mistress was of the society. I tried to compose myself in vain, not knowing how to dispose of either my legs or arms, nor how to shape my countenance, the eyes of the whole room being still upon me in a profound silence. My confusion at last was so great, that, without speaking, or being spoken to, I fled for it, and left the assembly to treat me at their discretion. A lecture from you upon these inhuman distinctions in a free nation will, I doubt not, prevent the like evils for the future, and make it, as we say, as cheap sitting as standing.
    "I am, with the greatest respect, Sir,
        "Your most humble, and
            "Most obedient servant,
                "J. R.
"Oct. 9.

"P.S.—I had almost forgot to inform you that a fair young lady sat in an armless chair upon my right hand, with manifest discontent in her looks."

Soon after the receipt of this epistle, I heard a very gentle knock at my door. My maid went down and brought up word "that a tall, lean, black man, well dressed, who said he had not the honour to be acquainted with me, desired to be admitted." I bid her show him up, met him at my chamber-door, and then fell back a few paces. He approached me with great respect, and told me, with a low voice, "he was the gentleman that had been seated upon the round stool." I immediately recollected that there was a joint-stool in my chamber, which I was afraid he might take for an instrument of distinction, and therefore winked at my boy to carry it into my closet. I then took him by the hand, and led him to the upper end of my room, where I placed him in my great elbow-chair, at the same time drawing another without arms to it for myself to sit by him. I then asked him, "at what time this misfortune befell him?" He answered, "Between the hours of seven and eight in the evening." I further demanded of him what he had ate or drank that day? He replied, "Nothing but a dish of water-gruel with a few plums in it." In the next place, I felt his pulse, which was very low and languishing. These circumstances confirmed me in an opinion, which I had entertained upon the first reading of his letter, that the

20

gentleman was far gone in the spleen. I therefore advised him to rise the next morning, and plunge into the cold bath, there to remain under water till he was almost drowned. This I ordered him to repeat six days successively; and on the seventh to repair at the wonted hour to my Lady Haughty's, and to acquaint me afterwards with what he shall meet with there: and particularly to tell me, whether he shall think they stared upon him so much as the time before. The gentleman smiled; and, by his way of talking to me, showed himself a man of excellent sense in all particulars, unless when a cane-chair, a round or a joint-stool, were spoken of. He opened his heart to me at the same time concerning several other grievances, such as being overlooked in public assemblies, having his bows unanswered, being helped last at table, and placed at the back part of a coach, with many other distresses, which have withered his countenance, and worn him to a skeleton. Finding him a man of reason, I entered into the bottom of his distemper. "Sir," said I, "there are more of your constitution in this island of Great Britain than in any other part of the world: and I beg the favour of you to tell me whether you do not observe that you meet with most affronts in rainy days?" He answered candidly, "that he had long observed, that people were less saucy in sunshine than in cloudy weather." Upon which I told him plainly, "his distemper was the spleen; and that though the world was very ill-natured, it was not so bad as he believed it." I further assured him, "that his use of the cold bath, with a course of *steel* which I should prescribe him, would certainly cure most of his acquaintance of their rudeness, ill-behaviour, and impertinence." My patient smiled and promised to observe my prescriptions, not forgetting to give me an account of their operation.

VII.—THE DREAM OF FAME.

From my own Apartment, October 14.

There are two kinds of immortality, that which the soul really enjoys after this life, and that imaginary existence by which men live in their fame and reputation. The best and greatest actions have proceeded from the prospect of the one or the other of these; but my design is to treat only of those who have chiefly proposed to themselves the latter as the principal reward of their labours. It was for this reason that I excluded from my Tables of Fame all the great founders and votaries of religion; and it is for this reason also that I am more than ordinarily anxious to do justice to the persons of whom I am now going to speak, for, since fame was the only end of all their enterprises and studies, a man cannot be too scrupulous in allotting them their due proportion of it. It was this consideration which made me call the whole body of the learned to my assistance; to many of whom I must own my obligations for the catalogues of illustrious persons which they have sent me in upon this occasion. I yesterday employed the whole afternoon in comparing them with each other, which made so strong an impression upon my imagination, that they broke my sleep for the first part of the following night, and at length threw me into a very agreeable vision, which I shall beg leave to describe in all its particulars.

I dreamed that I was conveyed into a wide and boundless plain, that was covered with prodigious multitudes of people, which no man could number. In the midst of it there stood a mountain, with its head above the clouds. The sides were extremely steep, and of such a particular structure, that no creature which was not made in a human figure could possibly ascend it. On a sudden there was heard from the top of it a sound like that of a trumpet, but so exceeding sweet and harmonious, that it filled the hearts of those who heard it with raptures, and gave such high and delightful sensations, as seemed to animate and raise human nature above itself. This made me very much amazed to find so very few in that innumerable multitude who had ears fine enough to hear or relish this music with pleasure; but my wonder abated when, upon looking round me, I saw most of them attentive to three Syrens, clothed like goddesses, and distinguished by the names of Sloth, Ignorance, and Pleasure. They were seated on three rocks, amidst a beautiful variety of groves, meadows, and rivulets that lay on the borders of the mountain. While this base and grovelling multitude of different nations, ranks, and ages were listening to these delusive deities, those of a more erect aspect and exalted spirit separated themselves from the rest, and marched in great bodies towards the mountain from whence they heard the sound, which still grew sweeter the more they listened to it.

On a sudden methought this select band sprang forward, with a resolution to climb the ascent, and follow the call of that heavenly music. Every one took something with him that he thought might be of assistance to him in his march. Several had their swords drawn, some carried rolls of paper in their hands, some had compasses, others quadrants, others telescopes, and others pencils. Some had laurels on their heads, and others buskins on their legs; in short, there was scarce any instrument of a mechanic art, or liberal science, which was not made of use on this occasion. My good demon, who stood at my right hand during this course of the whole vision, observing in me a burning desire to join that glorious company, told me, "he highly approved that generous ardour with which I seemed transported; but at the same time advised me to cover my face with a mask all the while I was to labour on the ascent." I took his counsel, without inquiring into his reasons. The whole body now broke into different parties, and began to climb the precipice by ten thousand different paths. Several got into little alleys, which did not reach far up the hill before they ended, and led no further; and I observed that most of the artizans, which considerably diminished our number, fell into these paths.

We left another considerable body of adventurers behind us who thought they had discovered byways up the hill, which proved so very intricate and perplexed, that after having advanced in them a little they were quite lost among the several turns and windings; and though they were as active as any in their motions, they made but little progress in the ascent. These, as my guide informed me, were men of subtle tempers, and puzzled politics, who would supply the place of real wisdom with cunning and artifice. Among those who were far advanced in their way there were some that by one false step fell backward, and lost more ground in a moment, than they had gained for many hours, or could be ever able to recover. We were now advanced very high, and observed that all the different paths which ran about the sides of the mountain began to meet in two great roads, which insensibly gathered the whole multitude of travellers into two great bodies. At a little distance from the entrance of each road there stood a hideous phantom, that opposed our further passage. One of these apparitions had his right hand filled with darts, which he brandished in the face of all who came up that way. Crowds ran back at the appearance of it, and cried out, "Death!" The spectre that guarded the other road was Envy. She was not armed with weapons of destruction, like the former, but by dreadful hissings, noises of reproach, and a horrid distracted laughter; she appeared more frightful than Death itself, insomuch that abundance of our company were discouraged from passing any further, and some appeared ashamed of having come so far. As for myself, I must confess my heart shrunk within me at the sight of these ghastly appearances; but, on a sudden, the voice of the trumpet came more full upon us, so that we felt a new resolution reviving in us, and in proportion as this resolution grew the terrors before us seemed to vanish. Most of the company, who had swords in their hands, marched on with great spirit, and an air of defiance, up the road that was commanded by Death; while others, who had thought and contemplation in their looks, went forward in a more composed manner up the road possessed by Envy. The way above these apparitions grew smooth and uniform, and was so delightful, that the travellers went on with pleasure, and in a little time arrived at the top of the mountain. They here began to breathe a delicious kind of ether, and saw all the fields about them covered with a kind of purple light, that made them reflect with satisfaction on their past toils, and diffused a secret joy through the whole assembly, which showed itself in every look and feature. In the midst of these happy fields there stood a palace of a very glorious structure. It had four great folding-doors that faced the four several quarters of the world. On the top of it was enthroned the goddess of the mountain, who smiled upon her votaries, and sounded the silver trumpet which had called them up, and cheered them in their passage to her palace.

They had now formed themselves into several divisions, a band of historians taking their stations at each door, according to the persons whom they were to introduce.

On a sudden the trumpet, which had hitherto sounded only a march, or a point of war, now swelled all its notes into triumph and exultation. The whole fabric shook, and the doors flew open. The first who stepped forward was a beautiful and blooming hero, and, as I heard by the murmurs round me, Alexander the Great. He was conducted by a crowd of historians. The person who immediately walked before him was remarkable for an embroidered garment, who, not being well acquainted with the place, was conducting him to an apartment appointed for the reception of fabulous heroes. The name of this false guide was Quintus Curtius. But Arrian and Plutarch, who knew better the avenues of this palace, conducted him into the great hall, and placed him at the upper end of the first table. My good demon, that I might see the whole ceremony, conveyed me to a corner of this room, where I might perceive all that passed without being seen myself. The next who entered was a charming virgin, leading in a venerable old man that was blind. Under her left arm she bore a harp, and on her head a garland. Alexander, who was very well acquainted with Homer, stood up at his entrance, and placed him on his right hand. The virgin, who it seems was one of the Nine Sisters that attended on the Goddess of Fame, smiled with an ineffable grace at their meeting, and retired.

Julius Caesar was now coming forward; and though most of the historians offered their service to introduce him, he left them at the door, and would have no conductor but himself.

The next who advanced was a man of a homely but cheerful aspect, and attended by persons of greater figure than any that appeared on this occasion. Plato was on his right hand, and Xenophon on his left. He bowed to Homer, and sat down by him. It was expected that Plato would himself have taken a place next to his master Socrates: but on a sudden there was heard a great clamour of disputants at the door, who appeared with Aristotle at the head of them. That philosopher, with some rudeness, but great strength of reason, convinced the whole table that a title to the fifth place was his due, and took it accordingly.

He had scarce sat down, when the same beautiful virgin that had introduced Homer brought in another, who hung back at the entrance, and would have excused himself, had not his modesty been overcome by the invitation of all who sat at the table. His guide and behaviour made me easily conclude it was Virgil. Cicero next appeared, and took his place. He had inquired at the door for Lucceius to introduce him, but not finding him there, he contented himself with the attendance of many other writers, who all, except Sallust, appeared highly pleased with the office.

We waited some time in expectation of the next worthy, who came in with a great retinue of historians, whose names I could not learn, most of them being natives of Carthage. The person thus conducted, who was Hannibal, seemed much disturbed, and could not forbear complaining to the board of the affronts he had met with among the Roman historians, "who attempted," says he, "to carry me into the

24

subterraneous apartment, and perhaps would have done it, had it not been for the impartiality of this gentleman," pointing to Polybius, "who was the only person, except my own countrymen, that was willing to conduct me hither."

The Carthaginian took his seat, and Pompey entered, with great dignity in his own person, and preceded by several historians. Lucan the poet was at the head of them, who, observing Homer and Virgil at the table, was going to sit down himself, had not the latter whispered him that whatever pretence he might otherwise have had, he forfeited his claim to it by coming in as one of the historians. Lucan was so exasperated with the repulse, that he muttered something to himself, and was heard to say that since he could not have a seat among them himself, he would bring in one who alone had more merit than their whole assembly: upon which he went to the door and brought in Cato of Utica. That great man approached the company with such an air that showed he contemned the honour which he laid a claim to. Observing the seat opposite to Caesar was vacant, he took possession of it, and spoke two or three smart sentences upon the nature of precedency, which, according to him, consisted not in place, but in intrinsic merit: to which he added, "that the most virtuous man, wherever he was seated, was always at the upper end of the table." Socrates, who had a great spirit of raillery with his wisdom, could not forbear smiling at a virtue which took so little pains to make itself agreeable. Cicero took the occasion to make a long discourse in praise of Cato, which he uttered with much vehemence. Caesar answered him with a great deal of seeming temper, but, as I stood at a great distance from them, I was not able to hear one word of what they said. But I could not forbear taking notice that in all the discourse which passed at the table a word or nod from Homer decided the controversy.

After a short pause Augustus appeared, looking round him, with a serene and affable countenance, upon all the writers of his age, who strove among themselves which of them should show him the greatest marks of gratitude and respect. Virgil rose from the table to meet him; and though he was an acceptable guest to all, he appeared more such to the learned than the military worthies.

The next man astonished the whole table with his appearance. He was slow, solemn, and silent in his behaviour, and wore a raiment curiously wrought with hieroglyphics. As he came into the middle of the room, he threw back the skirt of it, and discovered a golden thigh. Socrates, at the sight of it, declared against keeping company with any who were not made of flesh and blood, and, therefore, desired Diogenes the Laertian to lead him to the apartment allotted for fabulous heroes and worthies of dubious existence. At his going out he told them, "that they did not know whom they dismissed; that he was now Pythagoras, the first of philosophers, and that formerly he had been a very brave man at the Siege of Troy." "That may be true," said Socrates, "but you forget that you have likewise been a very great harlot in your time." This exclusion made way for Archimedes, who came forward with a scheme of mathematical figures in his hand, among which I observed a cone and a cylinder.

Seeing this table full, I desired my guide, for variety, to lead me to the fabulous apartment, the roof of which was painted with Gorgons, Chimeras, and Centaurs, with many other emblematical figures, which I wanted both time and skill to unriddle. The first table was almost full. At the upper end sat Hercules, leaning an arm upon his club; on his right hand were Achilles and Ulysses, and between them AEneas; on his left were Hector, Theseus, and Jason: the lower end had Orpheus, AEsop, Phalaris, and Musaeus. The ushers seemed at a loss for a twelfth man, when, methought, to my great joy and surprise, I heard some at the lower end of the table mention Isaac Bickerstaff; but those of the upper end received it with disdain, and said, "if they must have a British worthy, they would have Robin Hood!"

While I was transported with the honour that was done me, and burning with envy against my competitor, I was awakened by the noise of the cannon which were then fired for the taking of *Mons*. I should have been very much troubled at being thrown out of so pleasing a vision on any other occasion; but thought it an agreeable change, to have my thoughts diverted from the greatest among the dead and fabulous heroes to the most famous among the real and the living.

VIII.—LOVE AND SORROW.

From my own Apartment, October 17.

After the mind has been employed on contemplations suitable to its greatness, it is unnatural to run into sudden mirth or levity; but we must let the soul subside, as it rose, by proper degrees. My late considerations of the ancient heroes impressed a certain gravity upon my mind, which is much above the little gratification received from starts of humour and fancy, and threw me into a pleasing sadness. In this state of thought I have been looking at the fire, and in a pensive manner reflecting upon the great misfortunes and calamities incident to human life, among which there are none that touch so sensibly as those which befall persons who eminently love, and meet with fatal interruptions of their happiness when they least expect it. The piety of children to parents, and the affection of parents to their children, are the effects of instinct; but the affection between lovers and friends is founded on reason and choice, which has always made me think the sorrows of the latter much more to be pitied than those of the former. The contemplation of distresses of this sort softens the mind of man, and makes the heart better. It extinguishes the seeds of envy and ill-will towards mankind, corrects the pride of prosperity, and beats down all that fierceness and insolence which are apt to get into the minds of the daring and fortunate.

For this reason the wise Athenians, in their theatrical performances, laid before the eyes of the people the greatest afflictions which could befall human life, and insensibly polished their tempers by such representations. Among the moderns, indeed, there has arisen a chimerical method of disposing the fortune of the persons represented, according to what they call poetical justice; and letting none be unhappy but those who deserve it. In such cases, an intelligent spectator, if he is concerned, knows he ought not to be so, and can learn nothing from such a tenderness, but that he is a weak creature, whose passions cannot follow the dictates of his understanding. It is very natural, when one is got into such a way of thinking, to recollect these examples of sorrow which have made the strongest impression upon our imaginations. An instance or two of such you will give me leave to communicate.

A young gentleman and lady of ancient and honourable houses in Cornwall had from their childhood entertained for each other a generous and noble passion, which had been long opposed by their friends, by reason of the inequality of their fortunes; but their constancy to each other, and obedience to those on whom they depended, wrought so much upon their relations, that these celebrated lovers were at length joined in marriage. Soon after their nuptials the bridegroom was obliged to go into a foreign country, to take care of a considerable fortune, which was left him by a relation, and came very opportunely to improve their moderate circumstances. They received the congratulations of all the country on this occasion; and I remember it was a common sentence in everyone's mouth, "You see how faithful love is rewarded."

He took this agreeable voyage, and sent home every post fresh accounts of his success in his affairs abroad; but at last, though he designed to return with the next ship, he lamented in his letters that "business would detain him some time longer from home," because he would give himself the pleasure of an unexpected arrival.

The young lady, after the heat of the day, walked every evening on the sea-shore, near which she lived, with a familiar friend, her husband's kinswoman, and diverted herself with what objects they met there, or upon discourses of the future methods of life, in the happy change of their circumstances. They stood one evening on the shore together in a perfect tranquillity, observing the setting of the sun, the calm face of the deep, and the silent heaving of the waves, which gently rolled towards them, and broke at their feet, when at a distance her kinswoman saw something float on the waters, which she fancied was a chest, and with a smile told her, "she saw it first, and if it came ashore full of jewels she had a right to it." They both fixed their eyes upon it, and entertained themselves with the subject of the wreck, the cousin still asserting her right, but promising, "if it was a prize, to give her a very rich coral for the child which she was then expecting, provided she might be godmother." Their mirth soon abated when they observed upon the nearer approach that it was a human body. The young lady, who had a heart naturally filled with pity and compassion, made many melancholy reflections on the occasion. "Who knows," said she, "but this man may be the only hope and heir of a wealthy house; the darling of indulgent parents, who are now in impertinent mirth, and pleasing themselves with the thoughts of offering him a bride they had got ready for him? or, may not he be the master of a family that wholly depended upon his life? There may, for aught we know, be half-a-dozen fatherless children and a tender wife, now exposed to poverty by his death. What pleasure might he have promised himself in the different welcome he was to have from her and them! But let us go away; it is a dreadful sight! The best office we can do is to take care that the poor man, whoever he is, may be decently buried." She turned away, when the wave threw the carcass on the shore. The kinswoman immediately shrieked out, "Oh, my cousin!" and fell upon the ground. The unhappy wife went to help her friend, when she saw her own husband at her feet, and dropped in a swoon upon the body. An old woman, who had been the gentleman's nurse, came out about this time to call the ladies in to supper, and found her child, as she always called him, dead on the shore, her mistress and kinswoman both lying dead by him. Her loud lamentations, and calling her young master to life, soon awaked the friend from her trance, but the wife was gone for ever.

When the family and neighbourhood got together round the bodies, no one asked any question, but the objects before them told the story.

Incidents of this nature are the more moving when they are drawn by persons concerned in the catastrophe, notwithstanding they are often oppressed beyond the power of giving them in a distinct light, except we gather their sorrow from their inability to speak it.

I have two original letters, written both on the same day, which are to me exquisite in their different kinds. The occasion was this. A gentleman who had courted a most agreeable young woman, and won her heart, obtained also the consent of her father, to whom she was an only child. The old man had a fancy that they should be married in the same church where he himself was, in a village in Westmoreland, and made them set out while he was laid up with the gout at London. The bridegroom took only his man, the bride her maid: they had the most agreeable journey imaginable to the place of marriage, from whence the bridegroom writ the following letter to his wife's father:—

"Sir,

"After a very pleasant journey hither, we are preparing for the happy hour in which I am to be your son. I assure you the bride carries it, in the eye of the vicar who married you, much beyond her mother though he says your open sleeves, pantaloons, and shoulder-knot made a much better show than the finical dress I am in. However, I am contented to be the second fine man this village ever saw, and shall make it very merry before night, because I shall write myself from thence,

"Your most dutiful son,

"T. D.

"March 18, 1672.

"The bride gives her duty, and is as handsome as an angel. I am the happiest man breathing."

The villagers were assembling about the church, and the happy couple took a walk in a private garden. The bridegroom's man knew his master would leave the place on a sudden after the wedding, and seeing him draw his pistols the night before, took this opportunity to go into his chamber and charge them. Upon their return from the garden, they went into that room, and, after a little fond raillery on the subject of their courtship, the lover took up a pistol, which he knew he had unloaded the night before, and, presenting it to her, said, with the most graceful air, whilst she looked pleased at his agreeable flattery, "Now, madam, repent of all those cruelties you have been guilty of to me; consider, before you die, how often you have made a poor wretch freeze under your casement; you shall die, you tyrant, you shall die, with all those instruments of death and destruction about you, with that enchanting smile, those killing ringlets of your hair—" "Give fire!" said she, laughing. He did so, and shot her dead. Who can speak his condition? but he bore it so patiently as to call up his man. The poor wretch entered, and his master locked the door upon him. "Will," said he, "did you charge these pistols?" He answered, "Yes." Upon which, he shot him dead with that remaining. After this, amidst a thousand broken sobs, piercing groans, and distracted motions, he writ the following letter to the father of his dead mistress:—

"Sir,

"I, who two hours ago told you truly I was the happiest man alive am now the most miserable. Your daughter lies dead at my feet, killed by my hand, through a mistake of my man's charging my pistols unknown to me. Him I have murdered for it. Such is my wedding day. I will immediately follow my wife to her grave, but before I throw myself upon my sword, I command my distraction so far as to explain my story to you. I fear my heart will not keep together till I have stabbed it. Poor good old man! Remember, he that killed your daughter died for it. In the article of death, I give you my thanks and pray for you, though I dare not for myself. If it be possible, do not curse me."

IX.—LOVE AND REASON.

From my own Apartment, October 19.

It is my frequent practice to visit places of resort in this town where I am least known, to observe what reception my works meet with in the world, and what good effects I may promise myself from my labours, and it being a privilege asserted by Monsieur Montaigne, and others, of vain-glorious memory, that we writers of essays may talk of ourselves, I take the liberty to give an account of the remarks which I find are made by some of my gentle readers upon these my dissertations.

I happened this evening to fall into a coffee-house near the 'Change, where two persons were reading my account of the "Table of Fame."

The one of these was commenting as he read, and explaining who was meant by this and the other worthy as he passed on. I observed the person over against him wonderfully intent and satisfied with his explanation. When he came to Julius Caesar, who is said to have refused any conductor to the table: "No, no," said he, "he is in the right of it, he has money enough to be welcome wherever he comes;" and then whispered, "He means a certain colonel of the Trainbands." Upon reading that Aristotle made his claim with some rudeness, but great strength of reason; "Who can that be, so rough and so reasonable? It must be some Whig, I warrant you. There is nothing but party in these public papers." Where Pythagoras is said to have a golden thigh, "Ay, ay," said he, "he has money enough in his breeches; that is the alderman of our ward." You must know, whatever he read, I found he interpreted from his own way of life and acquaintance. I am glad my readers can construe for themselves these difficult points; but, for the benefit of posterity, I design, when I come to write my last paper of this kind, to make it an explanation of all my former. In that piece you shall have all I have commended with their proper names. The faulty characters must be left as they are, because we live in an age wherein vice is very general, and virtue very particular; for which reason the latter only wants explanation.

But I must turn my present discourse to what is of yet greater regard to me than the care of my writings; that is to say, the preservation of a lady's heart. Little did I think I should ever have business of this kind on my hands more; but, as little as any one who knows me would believe it, there is a lady at this time who professes love to me. Her passion and good humour you shall have in her own words.

"*Mr. Bickerstaff*,
    "I had formerly a very good opinion of myself; but it is now
withdrawn, and I have placed it upon you, Mr. Bickerstaff, for whom I am not
ashamed to declare I have a very great passion and tenderness. It is not for your
face, for that I never saw; your shape and height I am equally a stranger to; but your
understanding charms me, and I am lost if you do not dissemble a little love for me.
I am not without hopes; because I am not like the tawdry gay things that are fit only
to make bone-lace. I am neither childish-young, nor beldame-old, but, the world

says, a good agreeable woman.

"Speak peace to a troubled heart, troubled only for you; and in your next paper, let me find your thoughts of me.

"Do not think of finding out who I am, for, notwithstanding your interest in demons, they cannot help you either to my name, or a sight of my face; therefore, do not let them deceive you.

"I can bear no discourse, if you are not the subject; and believe me, I know more of love than you do of astronomy.

"Pray, say some civil things in return to my generosity, and you shall have my very best pen employed to thank you, and I will confirm it.

"I am your admirer,
        "*Maria.*"

There is something wonderfully pleasing in the favour of women; and this letter has put me in so good a humour, that nothing could displease me since I received it. My boy breaks glasses and pipes, and instead of giving him a knock on the pate, as my way is, for I hate scolding at servants, I only say, "Ah, Jack! thou hast a head, and so has a pin," or some such merry expression. But, alas! how am I mortified when he is putting on my fourth pair of stockings on these poor spindles of mine! "The fair one understands love better than I astronomy!" I am sure, without the help of that art, this poor meagre trunk of mine is a very ill habitation for love. She is pleased to speak civilly of my sense, but Ingenium male habitat is an invincible difficulty in cases of this nature. I had always, indeed, from a passion to please the eyes of the fair, a great pleasure in dress. Add to this, that I have writ songs since I was sixty, and have lived with all the circumspection of an old beau as I am. But my friend Horace has very well said: "Every year takes something from us;" and instructed me to form my pursuits and desires according to the stage of my life; therefore, I have no more to value myself upon, than that, I can converse with young people without peevishness, or wishing myself a moment younger. For which reason, when I am amongst them, I rather moderate than interrupt their diversions. But though I have this complacency, I must not pretend to write to a lady civil things, as Maria desires. Time was, when I could have told her, "I had received a letter from her fair hands; and that, if this paper trembled as she read it, it then best expressed its author," or some other gay conceit. Though I never saw her, I could have told her, "that good sense and good-humour smiled in her eyes; that constancy and good-nature dwelt in her heart; that beauty and good-breeding appeared in all her actions." When I was five-and-twenty, upon sight of one syllable, even wrong spelt, by a lady I never saw, I could tell her, "that her height was that which was fit for inviting our approach, and commanding our respect; that a smile sat on her lips, which prefaced her expressions before she uttered them, and her aspect prevented her speech. All she could say, though she had an infinite deal of wit, was but a repetition of what was expressed by her form; her form! which struck her beholders with ideas more moving and forcible than ever were inspired by music, painting, or eloquence." At this rate I panted in those days; but ah! sixty-three! I am very sorry I can only return the agreeable Maria a passion expressed rather from the head than the heart.

"*Dear madam,*

"You have already seen the best of me, and I so passionately love you that I desire we may never meet. If you will examine your heart, you will find that you join the man with the philosopher; and if you have that kind opinion of my sense as you pretend, I question not but you add to it complexion, air, and shape; but, dear Molly, a man in his grand climacteric is of no sex. Be a good girl, and conduct yourself with honour and virtue, when you love one younger than myself. I am, with the greatest tenderness, your innocent lover, I. B."

X.—A BUSINESS MEETING.

From my own Apartment, October 25.

When I came home last night my servant delivered me the following letter:

"*Sir,*
    "I have orders from Sir Harry Quickset, of Staffordshire,
Baronet, to acquaint you that his honour Sir Harry himself, Sir Giles Wheelbarrow,
Knight, Thomas Rentfree, Esquire, Justice of the Quorum, Andrew Windmill,
Esquire, and Mr. Nicholas Doubt, of the Inner Temple, Sir Harry's grandson, will
wait upon you at the hour of nine to-morrow morning, being Tuesday the twenty-
fifth of October, upon business which Sir Harry will impart to you by word of
mouth. I thought it proper to acquaint you beforehand so many persons of quality
came, that you might not be surprised therewith. Which concludes, though by many
years' absence since I saw you at Stafford, unknown, Sir, your most humble servant,
    "*John Thrifty.*
"October 24."

I received this message with less surprise than I believe Mr. Thrifty imagined; for I
knew the good company too well to feel any palpitations at their approach; but I was
in very great concern how I should adjust the ceremonial, and demean myself to all
these great men, who perhaps had not seen anything above themselves for these
twenty years last past. I am sure that is the case of Sir Harry. Besides which, I was
sensible that there was a great point in adjusting my behaviour to the simple esquire,
so as to give him satisfaction and not disoblige the justice of the quorum.

The hour of nine was come this morning, and I had no sooner set chairs, by the
steward's letter, and fixed my tea-equipage, but I heard a knock at my door, which
was opened, but no one entered; after which followed a long silence, which was
broke at last by, "Sir, I beg your pardon; I think I know better," and another voice,
"Nay, good Sir Giles—" I looked out from my window, and saw the good company
all with their hats off and arms spread, offering the door to each other. After many
offers, they entered with much solemnity, in the order Mr. Thrifty was so kind as to
name them to me. But they are now got to my chamber-door, and I saw my old
friend Sir Harry enter. I met him with all the respect due to so reverend a vegetable;
for you are to know that is my sense of a person who remains idle in the same place
for half a century. I got him with great success into his chair by the fire, without
throwing down any of my cups. The knight-bachelor told me "he had a great respect
for my whole family, and would, with my leave, place himself next to Sir Harry, at
whose right hand he had sat at every quarter-sessions these thirty years, unless he
was sick." The steward in the rear whispered the young templar, "That is true to my
knowledge." I had the misfortune, as they stood cheek by jowl, to desire the esquire
to sit down before the justice of the quorum, to the no small satisfaction of the
former, and resentment of the latter. But I saw my error too late, and got them as
soon as I could into their seats. "Well," said I, "gentlemen, after I have told you how
glad I am of this great honour, I am to desire you to drink a dish of tea." They

answered one and all, "that they never drank tea in a morning." "Not in a morning!" said I, staring round me; upon which the pert jackanapes, Nic Doubt, tipped me the wink, and put out his tongue at his grandfather. Here followed a profound silence, when the steward in his boots and whip proposed, "that we should adjourn to some public house, where everybody might call for what they pleased, and enter upon the business." We all stood up in an instant, and Sir Harry filed off from the left, very discreetly, countermarching behind the chairs towards the door. After him Sir Giles in the same manner. The simple esquire made a sudden start to follow, but the justice of the quorum whipped between upon the stand of the stairs. A maid, going up with coals, made us halt, and put us into such confusion that we stood all in a heap, without any visible possibility of recovering our order; for the young jackanapes seemed to make a jest of this matter, and had so contrived, by pressing amongst us under pretence of making way, that his grandfather was got into the middle, and he knew nobody was of quality to stir a step till Sir Harry moved first. We were fixed in this perplexity for some time, till we heard a very loud noise in the street, and Sir Harry asking what it was, I, to make them move, said it was fire. Upon this, all ran down as fast as they could, without order or ceremony, till we got into the street, where we drew up in very good order, and filed off down Sheer Lane; the impertinent templar driving us before him as in a string, and pointing to his acquaintance who passed by.

I must confess I love to use people according to their own sense of good breeding, and therefore whipped in between the justice and the simple esquire. He could not properly take this ill, but I overheard him whisper the steward, "that he thought it hard that a common conjuror should take place of him, though an elder esquire." In this order we marched down Sheer Lane, at the upper end of which I lodge.

When we came to Temple Bar, Sir Harry and Sir Giles got over, but a run of coaches kept the rest of us on this side the street. However, we all at last landed, and drew up in very good order before Ben Tooke's shop, who favoured our rallying with great humanity; from whence we proceeded again till we came to Dick's coffee-house, where I designed to carry them. Here we were at our old difficulty, and took up the street upon the same ceremony. We proceeded through the entry, and were so necessarily kept in order by the situation, that we were now got into the coffee-house itself, where, as soon as we arrived we repeated our civilities to each other, after which, we marched up to the high table, which has an ascent to it enclosed in the middle of the room. The whole house was alarmed at this entry, made up of persons of so much state and rusticity. Sir Harry called for a mug of ale and Dyer's Letter. The boy brought the ale in an instant, but said they did not take in the Letter. "No!" says Sir Harry, "then take back your mug; we are like indeed to have good liquor at this house!" Here the templar tipped me a second wink, and, if I had not looked very grave upon him, I found he was disposed to be very familiar with me. In short, I observed after a long pause, that the gentlemen did not care to enter upon business till after their morning draught, for which reason I called for a bottle of mum, and finding that had no effect upon them, I ordered a second and a third, after which Sir Harry reached over to me and told me in a low voice, "that the place was too public for business, but he would call upon me again to-morrow morning at my own lodgings, and bring some more friends with him."

XI.—DUELLO.

From my own Apartment, November 11.

I had several hints and advertisements from unknown hands, that some, who are enemies to my labours, design to demand the fashionable way of satisfaction for the disturbance my Lucubrations have given them. I confess, as things now stand, I do not know how to deny such inviters, and am preparing myself accordingly. I have bought pumps and foils, and am every morning practising in my chamber. My neighbour, the dancing-master, has demanded of me why I take this liberty, since I would not allow it him? but I answered, "His was an act of an indifferent nature, and mine of necessity." My late treatises against duels have so far disobliged the fraternity of the noble science of defence, that I can get none of them to show me so much as one pass. I am, therefore, obliged to learn by book; and have accordingly several volumes, wherein all the postures are exactly delineated. I must confess I am shy of letting people see me at this exercise, because of my flannel waistcoat, and my spectacles, which I am forced to fix on, the better to observe the posture of the enemy.

I have upon my chamber-walls drawn at full length the figures of all sorts of men, from eight foot to three foot two inches. Within this height, I take it, that all the fighting men of Great Britain are comprehended. But, as I push, I make allowances for my being of a lank and spare body, and have chalked out in every figure my own dimensions: for I scorn to rob any man of his life, or to take advantage of his breadth: therefore, I press purely in a line down from his nose, and take no more of him to assault than he has of me: for, to speak impartially, if a lean fellow wounds a fat one in any part to the right or left, whether it be in carte or in tierce, beyond the dimensions of the said lean fellow's own breadth, I take it to be murder, and such a murder as is below a gentleman to commit. As I am spare, I am also very tall, and behave myself with relation to that advantage with the same punctilio; and I am ready to stoop or stand, according to the stature of my adversary. I must confess I have had great success this morning, and have hit every figure round the room in a mortal part, without receiving the least hurt, except a little scratch by falling on my face, in pushing at one at the lower end of my chamber; but I recovered so quick, and jumped so nimbly into my guard, that, if he had been alive, he could not have hurt me. It is confessed I have writ against duels with some warmth; but in all my discourses I have not ever said that I knew how a gentleman could avoid a duel if he were provoked to it; and since that custom is now become a law, I know nothing but the legislative power, with new animadversions upon it, can put us in a capacity of denying challenges, though we are afterwards hanged for it. But, no more of this at present. As things stand, I shall put up no more affronts; and I shall be so far from taking ill words, that I will not take ill looks. I therefore, warn all hot young fellows not to look hereafter more terrible than their neighbours: for, if they stare at me with their hats cocked higher than other people, I will not bear it. Nay, I give warning to all people in general to look kindly at me, for I will bear no frowns, even from ladies; and if any woman pretends to look scornfully at me, I shall demand satisfaction of the next of kin of the masculine gender.

36

XII.—HAPPY MARRIAGE.

From my own Apartment, November 16.

There are several persons who have many pleasures and entertainments in their possession, which they do not enjoy. It is, therefore, a kind and good office to acquaint them with their own happiness, and turn their attention to such instances of their good fortune which they are apt to overlook. Persons in the married state often want such a monitor; and pine away their days, by looking upon the same condition in anguish and murmur, which carries with it in the opinion of others a complication of all the pleasures of life, and a retreat from its inquietudes.

I am led into this thought by a visit I made an old friend, who was formerly my school-fellow. He came to town last week with his family for the winter, and yesterday morning sent me word his wife expected me to dinner. I am, as it were, at home at that house, and every member of it knows me for their well-wisher. I cannot, indeed, express the pleasure it is to be met by the children with so much joy as I am when I go thither. The boys and girls strive who shall come first when they think it is I that am knocking at the door; and that child which loses the race to me runs back again to tell the father it is Mr. Bickerstaff. This day I was led in by a pretty girl, that we all thought must have forgot me, for the family has been out of town these two years. Her knowing me again was a mighty subject with us, and took up our discourse at the first entrance. After which they began to rally me upon a thousand little stories they heard in the country about my marriage to one of my neighbour's daughters. Upon which the gentleman, my friend, said, "Nay, if Mr. Bickerstaff marries a child of any of his old companions, I hope mine shall have the preference: there is Mrs. Mary is now sixteen, and would make him as fine a widow as the best of them. But I know him too well; he is so enamoured with the very memory of those who flourished in our youth, that he will not so much as look upon the modern beauties. I remember, old gentleman, how often you went home in a day to refresh your countenance and dress, when Teraminta reigned in your heart. As we came up in the coach, I repeated to my wife some of your verses on her." With such reflections on little passages, which happened long ago, we passed our time, during a cheerful and elegant meal. After dinner his lady left the room, as did also the children. As soon as we were alone, he took me by the hand; "Well, my good friend," says he, "I am heartily glad to see thee: I was afraid you would never have seen all the company that dined with you to-day again. Do not you think the good woman of the house a little altered, since you followed her from the play-house, to find out who she was for me?" I perceived a tear fall down his cheek as he spoke, which moved me not a little. But, to turn the discourse, said I, "She is not indeed quite that creature she was, when she returned me the letter I carried from you: and told me 'she hoped, as I was a gentleman, I would be employed no more to trouble her, who had never offended me; but would be so much the gentleman's friend as to dissuade him from a pursuit which he could never succeed in.' You may remember I thought her in earnest, and you were forced to employ your cousin Will, who made his sister get acquainted with her for you. You cannot expect her to be for ever fifteen." "Fifteen!" replied my good friend; "ah! you little understand, you that have lived a bachelor, how great, how exquisite a pleasure there is, in being really beloved! It is impossible, that the most beauteous face in nature should raise in me such pleasing ideas, as when I look upon that excellent woman. That fading in her countenance is chiefly caused by her watching with me, in my fever. This was followed by a fit of sickness, which had like to have carried her off last winter. I tell you sincerely, I have so many obligations to her, that I cannot, with any sort of moderation, think of her present state of health. But as to what you say of fifteen, she gives me every day pleasures beyond what I ever knew in the possession of her beauty, when I was in the vigour of youth. Every moment of her life brings me fresh instances of her complacency to my inclinations, and her prudence in regard to my fortune. Her face is to me much more beautiful than when I first saw it; there is no decay in any feature, which I cannot trace from the very instant it was occasioned by some anxious concern for my welfare and interests. Thus, at the same time, methinks, the love I conceived towards her for what she was, is heightened by my gratitude for what she is. The love of a wife is as much above the idle passion commonly called by that name, as the loud laughter of buffoons is inferior to the elegant mirth of gentlemen. Oh! she is an inestimable jewel. In her examination of her household affairs she shows a certain fearfulness to find a fault, which makes her servants obey her like children: and the meanest we have has an ingenuous shame for an offence, not always to be seen in children in other families. I speak freely to you, my old friend: ever since her sickness, things that gave me the quickest joy before turn now to a certain anxiety. As the children play in the next room, I know the poor things by their steps, and am considering what they must do, should they lose their mother in their tender years. The pleasure I used to take in telling my boy stories of the battles, and asking my girl questions about the disposal of her baby, and the gossiping of it, is turned into inward reflection and melancholy."

He would have gone on in this tender way, when the good lady entered, and, with an inexpressible sweetness in her countenance, told us "she had been searching her closet for something very good, to treat such an old friend as I was." Her husband's eyes sparkled with pleasure at the cheerfulness of her countenance; and I saw all his fears vanish in an instant. The lady observing something in our looks which showed we had been more serious than ordinary, and seeing her husband receive her with great concern under a forced cheerfulness, immediately guessed at what we had been talking of; and applying herself to me, said, with a smile, "Mr. Bickerstaff, do not believe a word of what he tells you. I shall still live to have you for my second, as I have often promised you, unless he takes more care of himself than he has done since his coming to town. You must know he tells me that he finds London is a much more healthy place than the country, for he sees several of his old acquaintants and school-fellows are here young fellows with fair full-bottomed periwigs. I could scarce keep him this morning from going out open-breasted." My friend, who is always extremely delighted with her agreeable humour, made her sit down with us. She did it with that easiness which is peculiar to women of sense; and to keep up the good humour she had brought in with her, turned her raillery upon me. "Mr. Bickerstaff, you remember you followed me one night from the play-house; suppose you should carry me thither to-morrow night, and lead me into the front box." This put us into a long field of discourse about the beauties, who were mothers to the present, and shined in the boxes twenty years ago. I told her, "I was glad she had transferred so many of her charms, and I did not question but her eldest daughter was within half a year of being a Toast."

We were pleasing ourselves with this fantastical preferment of the young lady, when on a sudden we were alarmed with the noise of a drum, and immediately entered my little godson to give me a point of war. His mother, between laughing and chiding, would have put him out of the room; but I would not part with him so. I found upon conversation with him, though he was a little noisy in his mirth, that the child had excellent parts, and was a great master of all the learning on the other side eight years old. I perceived him a very great historian in AEsop's Fables: but he frankly declared to me his mind, that he did not delight in that learning, because he did not believe they were true; for which reason I found he had very much turned his studies for about a twelve-month past, into the lives and adventures of Don Bellianis of Greece, Guy of Warwick, the Seven Champions, and other historians of that age. I could not but observe the satisfaction the father took in the forwardness of his son; and that these diversions might turn to some profit, I found the boy had made remarks which might be of service to him during the course of his whole life. He would tell you the mis-managements of John Hickathrift, find fault with the passionate temper in Bevis of Southampton, and loved Saint George for being the champion of England; and by this means had his thoughts insensibly moulded into the notions of discretion, virtue, and honour. I was extolling his accomplishments, when the mother told me that the little girl who led me in this morning was in her way a better scholar than he. "Betty," says she, "deals chiefly in fairies and sprites, and sometimes in a winter-night will terrify the maids with her accounts, till they are afraid to go up to bed."

I sat with them till it was very late, sometimes in merry, sometimes in serious, discourse, with this particular pleasure, which gives the only true relish to all conversation, a sense that every one of us liked each other. I went home, considering the different conditions of a married life and that of a bachelor; and I must confess it struck me with a secret concern, to reflect, that whenever I go off I shall leave no traces behind me. In this pensive mood I return to my family; that is to say, to my maid, my dog, and my cat, who only can be the better or worse for what happens to me.

XIII.—DEAD FOLK.

From my own Apartment, November 17.

It has cost me very much care and thought to marshal and fix the people under their proper denominations, and to range them according to their respective characters. These my endeavours have been received with unexpected success in one kind, but neglected in another; for though I have many readers, I have but few converts. This must certainly proceed from a false opinion, that what I write is designed rather to amuse and entertain than convince and instruct. I entered upon my Essays with a declaration that I should consider mankind in quite another manner than they had hitherto been represented to the ordinary world, and asserted that none but a useful life should be, with me, any life at all. But, lest this doctrine should have made this small progress towards the conviction of mankind, because it may appear to the unlearned light and whimsical, I must take leave to unfold the wisdom and antiquity of my first proposition in these my essays, to wit, that "every worthless man is a dead man." This notion is as old as Pythagoras, in whose school it was a point of discipline, that if among the Akoustikoi, * or probationers, there were any who grew weary of studying to be useful, and returned to an idle life, the rest were to regard them as dead, and upon their departing, to perform their obsequies and raise them tombs, with inscriptions, to warn others of the like mortality, and quicken them to resolutions of refining their souls above that wretched state. It is upon a like supposition that young ladies, at this very time, in Roman Catholic countries, are received into some nunneries with their coffins, and with the pomp of a formal funeral, to signify that henceforth they are to be of no further use, and consequently dead. Nor was Pythagoras himself the first author of this symbol, with whom, and with the Hebrews, it was generally received. Much more might be offered in illustration of this doctrine from sacred authority, which I recommend to my reader's own reflection; who will easily recollect, from places which I do not think fit to quote here, the forcible manner of applying the words dead and living to men, as they are good or bad.

* Anglicised version of the author's original Greek text.

I have, therefore, composed the following scheme of existence for the benefit both of the living and the dead; though chiefly for the latter, whom I must desire to read it with all possible attention. In the number of the dead I comprehend all persons, of what title or dignity soever, who bestow most of their time in eating and drinking, to support that imaginary existence of theirs which they call life; or in dressing and adorning those shadows and apparitions, which are looked upon by the vulgar as real men and women. In short, whoever resides in the world without having any business in it, and passes away an age without ever thinking on the errand for which he was sent hither, is to me a dead man to all intents and purposes, and I desire that he may be so reputed. The living are only those that are some way or other laudably employed in the improvement of their own minds, or for the advantage of others; and even among these, I shall only reckon into their lives that part of their time which has been spent in the manner above mentioned. By these means, I am afraid we shall

40

find the longest lives not to consist of many months, and the greatest part of the earth to be quite unpeopled. According to this system we may observe that some men are born at twenty years of age, some at thirty, some at threescore, and some not above an hour before they die; nay, we may observe multitudes that die without ever being born, as well as many dead persons that fill up the bulk of mankind, and make a better figure in the eyes of the ignorant, than those who are alive, and in their proper and full state of health. However, since there may be many good subjects, that pay their taxes, and live peaceably in their habitations, who are not yet born, or have departed this life several years since, my design is to encourage both to join themselves as soon as possible to the number of the living. For as I invite the former to break forth into being and become good for something, so I allow the latter a state of resuscitation, which I chiefly mention for the sake of a person who has lately published an advertisement, with several scurrilous terms in it, that do by no means become a dead man to give. It is my departed friend, John Partridge, who concludes the advertisement of his next year's almanack with the following note:

"Whereas it has been industriously given out by Bickerstaff, Esquire, and others, to prevent the sale of this year's almanack, that John Partridge is dead: this may inform all his loving countrymen, that he is still living in health, and they are knaves that reported it otherwise.
    "J. P."

- - - - -

From my own Apartment, November 25.

I have already taken great pains to inspire notions of honour and virtue into the people of this kingdom, and used all gentle methods imaginable, to bring those who are dead in idleness, folly, and pleasure, into life, by applying themselves to learning, wisdom, and industry. But, since fair means are ineffectual, I must proceed to extremities, and shall give my good friends, the Company of Upholders, full power to bury all such dead as they meet with, who are within my former descriptions of deceased persons. In the meantime the following remonstrance of that corporation I take to be very just.

"*Worthy sir,*
    "Upon reading your Tatler of Saturday last, by which we
received the agreeable news of so many deaths, we immediately ordered in a considerable quantity of blacks, and our servants have wrought night and day ever since to furnish out the necessaries for these deceased. But so it is, Sir, that of this vast number of dead bodies that go putrifying up and down the streets, not one of them has come to us to be buried. Though we should be loth to be any hindrance to our good friends the physicians, yet we cannot but take notice what infection Her Majesty's subjects are liable to from the horrible stench of so many corpses. Sir, we will not detain you; our case in short is this: Here are we embarked in this undertaking for the public good. Now, if people should be suffered to go on

unburied at this rate, there is an end of the usefullest manufactures and handicrafts of the kingdom; for where will be your sextons, coffin-makers, and plumbers? What will become of your embalmers, epitaph-mongers, and chief-mourners? We are loth to drive this matter any farther, though we tremble at the consequences of it; for if it shall be left to every dead man's discretion not to be buried till he sees his time, no man can say where that will end; but thus much we will take upon us to affirm, that such a toleration will be intolerable.

"What would make us easy in this matter is no more but that your Worship would be pleased to issue out your orders to ditto Dead to repair forthwith to our office, in order to their interment, where constant attendance shall be given to treat with all persons according to their quality, and the poor to be buried for nothing. And, for the convenience of such persons as are willing enough to be dead, but that they are afraid their friends and relations should know it, we have a back door into Warwick Street, from whence they may be interred with all secrecy imaginable, and without loss of time or hindrance of business. But in case of obstinacy, for we would gladly make a thorough riddance, we desire a farther power from your Worship, to take up such deceased as shall not have complied with your first orders wherever we meet them; and if, after that, there shall be complaints of any person so offending, let them lie at our doors.

"We are your Worship's till death,

"The *master* and *company* of *upholders.*

"P.S. We are ready to give in our printed proposals at large, and if your Worship approves of our undertaking, we desire the following advertisement may be inserted in your next paper:

"Whereas a commission of interment has been awarded against Doctor John Partridge, philomath, professor of physic and astrology, and whereas the said Partridge hath not surrendered himself, nor shown cause to the contrary: These are to certify that the Company of Upholders will proceed to bury him from Cordwainer's Hall, on Tuesday the twenty-ninth instant, where any six of his surviving friends, who still believe him to be alive, are desired to come prepared to hold up the pall.

"Note. We shall light away at six in the evening, there being to be a sermon.

"From our Office near the Haymarket, Nov. 23."

XIV.—THE WIFE DEAD.

Sheer Lane, December 30.

I was walking about my chamber this morning in a very gay humour, when I saw a coach stop at my door, and a youth about fifteen alighting out of it, who I perceived to be the eldest son of my bosom friend, that I gave some account of in a previous paper. I felt a sensible pleasure rising in me at the sight of him, my acquaintance having begun with his father when he was just such a stripling, and about that very age. When he came up to me, he took me by the hand, and burst into tears. I was extremely moved, and immediately said, "Child, how does your father do?" He began to reply, "My mother—" but could not go on for weeping. I went down with him into the coach, and gathered out of him, "That his mother was then dying; and that, while the holy man was doing the last offices to her, he had taken that time to come and call me to his father, who, he said, would certainly break his heart, if I did not go and comfort him." The child's discretion in coming to me of his own head, and the tenderness he showed for his parents would have quite overpowered me, had I not resolved to fortify myself for the seasonable performances of those duties which I owed to my friend. As we were going, I could not but reflect upon the character of that excellent woman, and the greatness of his grief for the loss of one who has ever been the support to him under all other afflictions. How, thought I, will he be able to bear the hour of her death, that could not, when I was lately with him, speak of a sickness, which was then past, without sorrow! We were now got pretty far into Westminster, and arrived at my friend's house. At the door of it I met Favonius, not without a secret satisfaction to find he had been there. I had formerly conversed with him at his house; and as he abounds with that sort of virtue and knowledge which makes religion beautiful, and never leads the conversation into the violence and rage of party disputes, I listened to him with great pleasure. Our discourse chanced to be upon the subject of death, which he treated with such a strength of reason, and greatness of soul, that, instead of being terrible, it appeared to a mind rightly cultivated, altogether to be contemned, or rather to be desired. As I met him at the door, I saw in his face a certain glowing of grief and humanity, heightened with an air of fortitude and resolution, which, as I afterwards found, had such an irresistible force, as to suspend the pains of the dying, and the lamentation of the nearest friends who attended her. I went up directly to the room where she lay, and was met at the entrance by my friend, who, notwithstanding his thoughts had been composed a little before, at the sight of me turned away his face and wept. The little family of children renewed the expressions of their sorrow according to their several ages and degrees of understanding. The eldest daughter was in tears, busied in attendance upon her mother; others were kneeling about the bedside: and what troubled me most, was, to see a little boy, who was too young to know the reason, weeping only because his sisters did. The only one in the room who seemed resigned and comforted was the dying person. At my approach to the bedside, she told me, with a low broken voice, "This is kindly done—take care of your friend—do not go from him!" She had before taken leave of her husband and children, in a manner proper for so solemn a parting, and with a gracefulness peculiar to a woman of her character. My heart was torn to pieces, to see the husband on one side suppressing and keeping down the swellings of his grief, for fear of disturbing her in her last moments; and the wife even at that time concealing the pains she endured, for fear of increasing his affliction. She kept her eyes upon him for some moments after she grew speechless, and soon after closed them for ever. In the moment of her departure, my friend, who had thus far commanded himself, gave a deep groan, and fell into a swoon by her bedside. The distraction of the children, who thought they saw both their parents expiring together, and now lying dead before them, would have melted the hardest heart; but they soon perceived their father recover, whom I helped to remove into another room, with a resolution to accompany him till the first pangs of his affliction were abated. I knew consolation would now be impertinent; and, therefore, contented myself to sit by him, and condole with him in silence. For I shall here use the method of an ancient author, who in one of his epistles, relating the virtues and death of Macrinus's wife, expresses himself thus: "I shall suspend my advice to this best of friends, till he is made capable of receiving it by those three great remedies (necessitas ipsa, dies longa, et satietas doloris), the necessity of submission, length of time, and satiety of grief."

In the meantime, I cannot but consider, with much commiseration, the melancholy state of one who has had such a part of himself torn from him, and which he misses in every circumstance of life. His condition is like that of one who has lately lost his right arm, and is every moment offering to help himself with it. He does not appear to himself the same person in his house, at his table, in company, or in retirement; and loses the relish of all the pleasures and diversions that were before entertaining to him by her participation of them. This additional satisfaction, from the taste of pleasures in the society of one we love, is admirably described in Milton, who represents Eve, though in Paradise itself, no further pleased with the beautiful objects around her, than as she sees them in company with Adam, in that passage so inexpressibly charming:

"With thee conversing, I forget all time;
All seasons, and their change; all please alike.
Sweet is the breath of morn, her rising sweet
With charm of earliest birds; pleasant the sun,
When first on this delightful land he spreads
His orient beams, on herb, tree, fruit, and flower,
Glistering with dew; fragrant the fertile earth
After short showers; and sweet the coming on
Of grateful evening mild; the silent night,
With this her solemn bird, and this fair moon,
And these the gems of Heaven, her starry train.
But neither breath of morn when she ascends
With charm of earliest birds; nor rising sun
On this delightful land; nor herb, fruit, flower,
Glistering with dew; nor fragrance after showers;
Nor grateful evening mild; nor silent night,
With this her solemn bird, nor walk by moon,
Or glittering star-light, without thee is sweet."

44

The variety of images in this passage is infinitely pleasing; and the recapitulation of each particular image, with a little varying of the expression, makes one of the finest turns of words that I have ever seen: which I rather mention because Mr. Dryden has said, in his preface to Juvenal, that he could meet with no turn of words in Milton.

It may further be observed, that though the sweetness of these verses has something in it of a pastoral, yet it excels the ordinary kind, as much as the scene of it is above an ordinary field or meadow. I might here, as I am accidentally led into this subject, show several passages in Milton that have as excellent turns of this nature as any of our English poets whatsoever; but shall only mention that which follows, in which he describes the fallen angels engaged in the intricate disputes of predestination, free-will, and fore-knowledge; and, to humour the perplexity, makes a kind of labyrinth in the very words that describe it.

"Others apart sat on a hill retired,
In thoughts more elevate, and reasoned high
Of providence, fore-knowledge, will, and fate,
Fixed fate, free-will, fore-knowledge absolute,
And found no end, in wandering mazes lost."

XV.—THE CLUB AT "THE TRUMPET."

Sheer Lane, February 10, 1710.

After having applied my mind with more than ordinary attention to my studies, it is my usual custom to relax and unbend it in the conversation of such as are rather easy than shining companions. This I find particularly necessary for me before I retire, to rest, in order to draw my slumbers upon me by degrees, and fall asleep insensibly. This is the particular use I make of a set of heavy honest men, with whom I have passed many hours with much indolence, though not with great pleasure. Their conversation is a kind of preparative for sleep; it takes the mind down from its abstractions, leads it into the familiar traces of thought, and lulls it into that state of tranquillity, which is the condition of a thinking man, when he is but half-awake. After this, my reader will not be surprised to hear the account which I am about to give of a club of my own contemporaries, among whom I pass two or three hours every evening. This I look upon as taking my first nap before I go to bed. The truth of it is, I should think myself unjust to posterity, as well as to the society at "The Trumpet," of which I am a member, did not I in some part of my writings give an account of the persons among whom I have passed almost a sixth part of my time for these last forty years. Our club consisted originally of fifteen; but, partly by the severity of the law in arbitrary times, and partly by the natural effects of old age, we are at present reduced to a third part of that number: in which, however, we have this consolation that the best company is said to consist of five persons. I must confess, besides the aforementioned benefit which I meet with in the conversation of this select society, I am not the less pleased with the company, in that I find myself the greatest wit among them, and am heard as their oracle in all points of learning and difficulty.

Sir Jeoffery Notch, who is the oldest of the club, has been in possession of the right-hand chair time out of mind, and is the only man among us that has the liberty of stirring the fire. This our foreman is a gentleman of an ancient family, that came to a great estate some years before he had discretion, and run it out in hounds, horses, and cock-fighting; for which reason he looks upon himself as an honest, worthy gentleman, who has had misfortunes in the world, and calls every thriving man a pitiful upstart.

Major Matchlock is the next senior, who served in the last civil wars, and has all the battles by heart. He does not think any action in Europe worth talking of, since the fight of Marston Moor; and every night tells us of his having been knocked off his horse at the rising of the London apprentices; for which he is in great esteem among us.

Honest old Dick Reptile is the third of our society. He is a good-natured indolent man, who speaks little himself, but laughs at our jokes; and brings his young nephew along with him, a youth of eighteen years old, to show him good company, and give him a taste of the world. This young fellow sits generally silent; but whenever he opens his mouth, or laughs at anything that passes, he is constantly told by his uncle, after a jocular manner, "Ay, ay, Jack, you young men think us fools; but we old men know you are."

The greatest wit of our company, next to myself, is a Bencher, of the neighbouring Inn, who in his youth frequented the ordinaries about Charing Cross, and pretends to have been intimate with Jack Ogle. He has about ten distichs of Hudibras without book, and never leaves the club till he has applied them all. If any modern wit be mentioned, or any town-frolic spoken of, he shakes his head at the dulness of the present age, and tells us a story of Jack Ogle.

For my own part, I am esteemed among them, because they see I am something respected by others; though at the same time I understand by their behaviour, that I am considered by them as a man of a great deal of learning, but no knowledge of the world; insomuch, that the Major sometimes, in the height of his military pride, calls me the philosopher; and Sir Jeoffery, no longer ago than last night, upon a dispute what day of the month it was then in Holland, pulled his pipe out of his mouth, and cried, "What does the Scholar say to it?"

Our club meets precisely at six o'clock in the evening; but I did not come last night till half an hour after seven, by which means I escaped the battle of Naseby, which the Major usually begins at about three-quarters after six. I found also, that my good friend the Bencher had already spent three of his distichs; and only waiting an opportunity to hear a sermon spoken of that he might introduce the couplet where "a stick" rhymes to "ecclesiastic." At my entrance into the room, they were naming a red petticoat and a cloak, by which I found that the Bencher had been diverting them with a story of Jack Ogle.

I had no sooner taken my seat, but Sir Jeoffery, to show his good will towards me, gave me a pipe of his own tobacco, and stirred up the fire. I look upon it as a point of morality, to be obliged by those who endeavour to oblige me; and therefore, in requital for his kindness, and to set the conversation a-going, I took the best occasion I could to put him upon telling us the story of old Gantlett, which he always does with very particular concern. He traced up his descent on both sides for several generations, describing his diet and manner of life, with his several battles, and particularly that in which he fell. This Gantlett was a game-cock, upon whose head the knight, in his youth, had won five hundred pounds, and lost two thousand. This naturally set the Major upon the account of Edge-hill fight, and ended in a duel of Jack Ogle's.

Old Reptile was extremely attentive to all that was said, though it was the same he had heard every night for these twenty years, and upon all occasions winked upon his nephew to mind what passed.

This may suffice to give the world a taste of our innocent conversation, which we spun out till about ten of the clock, when my maid came with a lantern to light me home. I could not but reflect with myself, as I was going out, upon the talkative humour of old men, and the little figure which that part of life makes in one who cannot employ this natural propensity in discourses which would make him venerable. I must own, it makes me very melancholy in company, when I hear a young man begin a story; and have often observed, that one of a quarter of an hour long in a man of five-and-twenty, gathers circumstances every time he tells it, till it grows into a long Canterbury tale of two hours by that time he is three-score.

The only way of avoiding such a trifling and frivolous old age is to lay up in our way to it such stores of knowledge and observation as may make us useful and agreeable in our declining years. The mind of man in a long life will become a magazine of wisdom or folly, and will consequently discharge itself in something impertinent or improving. For which reason, as there is nothing more ridiculous than an old trifling story-teller, so there is nothing more venerable than one who has turned his experience to the entertainment and advantage of mankind.

In short, we, who are in the last stage of life, and are apt to indulge ourselves in talk, ought to consider if what we speak be worth being heard, and endeavour to make our discourse like that of Nestor, which Homer compares to the flowing of honey for its sweetness.

I am afraid I shall be thought guilty of this excess I am speaking of, when I cannot conclude without observing that Milton certainly thought of this passage in Homer, when, in his description of an eloquent spirit, he says—

"His tongue dropped manna."

XVI.—A VERY PRETTY POET.

Will's Coffee-house, April 24.

I yesterday came hither about two hours before the company generally make their appearance, with a design to read over all the newspapers; but, upon my sitting down, I was accosted by Ned Softly, who saw me from a corner in the other end of the room, where I found he had been writing something. "Mr. Bickerstaff," says he, "I observe by a late paper of yours, that you and I are just of a humour; for you must know, of all impertinences, there is nothing which I so much hate as news. I never read a gazette in my life; and never trouble my head about our armies, whether they win or lose, or in what part of the world they lie encamped." Without giving me time to reply, he drew a paper of verses out of his pocket, telling me, "that he had something which would entertain me more agreeably, and that he would desire my judgment upon every line, for that we had time enough before us till the company came in."

Ned Softly is a very pretty poet, and a great admirer of easy lines. Waller is his favourite: and as that admirable writer has the best and worst verses of any among our great English poets, Ned Softly has got all the bad ones without book, which he repeats upon occasion, to show his reading, and garnish his conversation. Ned is indeed a true English reader, incapable of relishing the great and masterly strokes of this art; but wonderfully pleased with the little Gothic ornaments of epigrammatical conceits, turns, points, and quibbles, which are so frequent in the most admired of our English poets, and practised by those who want genius and strength to represent, after the manner of the ancients, simplicity in its natural beauty and perfection.

Finding myself unavoidably engaged in such a conversation, I was resolved to turn my pain into a pleasure and to divert myself as well as I could with so very odd a fellow. "You must understand," says Ned, "that the sonnet I am going to read to you was written upon a lady, who showed me some verses of her own making, and is, perhaps, the best poet of our age. But you shall hear it."

Upon which he began to read as follows:

"*To Mira, on her incomparable poems.*

1.
   "When dressed in laurel wreaths you shine,
    And tune your soft melodious notes,
  You seem a sister of the Nine,
    Or Phoebus' self in petticoats.

2.
   "I fancy, when your song you sing,
    Your song you sing with so much art,

Your pen was plucked from Cupid's wing;
    For, ah! it wounds me like his dart."

"Why," says I, "this is a little nosegay of conceits, a very lump of salt: every verse has something in it that piques; and then the dart in the last line is certainly as pretty a sting in the tail of an epigram, for so I think you critics call it, as ever entered into the thought of a poet." "Dear Mr. Bickerstaff," says he, shaking me by the hand, "everybody knows you to be a judge of these things; and, to tell you truly, I read over Roscommon's translation of Horace's 'Art of Poetry' three several times before I sat down to write the sonnet which I have shown you. But you shall hear it again, and pray observe every line of it; for not one of them shall pass without your approbation.

    "'When dressed in laurel wreaths you shine,'

"That is," says he, "when you have your garland on; when you are writing verses." To which I replied, "I know your meaning: a metaphor!" "The same," said he, and went on.

    "'And tune your soft melodious notes,'

"Pray observe the gliding of that verse; there is scarce a consonant in it: I took care to make it run upon liquids. Give me your opinion of it." "Truly," said I, "I think it as good as the former." "I am very glad to hear you say so," says he; "but mind the next.

    "'You seem a sister of the Nine,

"That is," says he, "you seem a sister of the Muses; for, if you look into ancient authors, you will find it was their opinion that there were nine of them." "I remember it very well," said I; "but pray proceed."

    "'Or Phoebus' self in petticoats.'

"Phoebus," says he, "was the god of Poetry. These little instances, Mr. Bickerstaff, show a gentleman's reading. Then to take off from the air of learning, which Phoebus and the Muses had given to this first stanza, you may observe, how it falls all of a sudden into the familiar; 'in petticoats!'

    "'Or Phoebus' self in petticoats.'"

"Let us now," says I, "enter upon the second stanza; I find the first line is still a continuation of the metaphor.

    "'I fancy when your song you sing.'"

"It is very right," says he; "but pray observe the turn of words in those two lines. I was a whole hour in adjusting of them, and have still a doubt upon me whether in the second line it should be, 'Your song you sing; or, You sing your song?' You shall hear them both:

"'I fancy, when your song you sing,
Your song you sing with so much art,'

or,

"'I fancy, when your song you sing,
You sing your song with so much art.'"

"Truly," said I, "the turn is so natural either way, that you have made me almost giddy with it." "Dear sir," said he, grasping me by the hand, "you have a great deal of patience; but pray what do you think of the next verse?

"'Your pen was plucked from Cupid's wing.'"

"Think!" says I; "I think you have made Cupid look like a little goose." "That was my meaning," says he: "I think the ridicule is well enough hit off. But we come now to the last, which sums up the whole matter.

"'For, ah! it wounds me like his dart.'

"Pray how do you like that Ah! doth it not make a pretty figure in that place? Ah!— it looks as if I felt the dart, and cried out at being pricked with it.

"'For, ah! it wounds me like his dart.'

"My friend Dick Easy," continued he, "assured me, he would rather have written that Ah! than to have been the author of the Æneid. He indeed objected, that I made Mira's pen like a quill in one of the lines, and like a dart in the other. But as to that—" "Oh! as to that," says I, "it is but supposing Cupid to be like a porcupine, and his quills and darts will be the same thing." He was going to embrace me for the hint; but half a dozen critics coming into the room, whose faces he did not like, he conveyed the sonnet into his pocket, and whispered me in the ear, "he would show it me again as soon as his man had written it over fair."

XVII.—FATHERLY CARE.

From my own Apartment, June 23.

Having lately turned my thoughts upon the consideration of the behaviour of parents to children in the great affair of marriage, I took much delight in turning over a bundle of letters which a gentleman's steward in the country had sent me some time ago. This parcel is a collection of letters written by the children of the family to which he belongs to their father, and contain all the little passages of their lives, and the new ideas they received as the years advanced. There is in them an account of their diversions as well as their exercises; and what I thought very remarkable is, that two sons of the family, who now make considerable figures in the world, gave omens of that sort of character which they now bear in the first rudiments of thought which they show in their letters. Were one to point out a method of education, one could not, methinks, frame one more pleasing or improving than this; where the children get a habit of communicating their thoughts and inclinations to their best friend with so much freedom, that he can form schemes for their future life and conduct from an observation of their tempers; and by that means be early enough in choosing their way of life, to make them forward in some art or science at an age when others have not determined what profession to follow. As to the persons concerned in this packet I am speaking of, they have given great proofs of the force of this conduct of their father in the effect it has upon their lives and manners. The older, who is a scholar, showed from his infancy a propensity to polite studies, and has made a suitable progress in literature; but his learning is so well woven into his mind, that from the impressions of it, he seems rather to have contracted a habit of life than manner of discourse. To his books he seems to owe a good economy in his affairs, and a complacency in his manners, though in others that way of education has commonly a quite different effect. The epistles of the other son are full of accounts of what he thought most remarkable in his reading. He sends his father for news the last noble story he had read. I observe he is particularly touched with the conduct of Codrus, who plotted his own death, because the oracle had said, if he were not killed, the enemy should prevail over his country. Many other incidents in his little letters give omens of a soul capable of generous undertakings; and what makes it the more particular is, that this gentleman had, in the present war, the honour and happiness of doing an action for which only it was worth coming into the world. Their father is the most intimate friend they have; and they always consult him rather than any other, when any error has happened in their conduct through youth and inadvertency. The behaviour of this gentleman to his sons has made his life pass away with the pleasures of a second youth; for as the vexations which men receive from their children hasten the approach of age, and double the force of years; so the comforts which they reap from them, are balm to all other sorrows, and disappoint the injuries of time. Parents of children repeat their lives in their offspring; and their concern for them is so near, that they feel all their sufferings and enjoyments as much as if they regarded their own proper persons. But it is generally so far otherwise, that the common race of 'squires in this kingdom use their sons as persons that are waiting only for their funerals, and spies upon their health and happiness; as indeed they are, by their own making them such. In cases where a man

52

takes the liberty after this manner to reprehend others, it is commonly said, Let him look at home. I am sorry to own it; but there is one branch of the house of the Bickerstaffs who have been as erroneous in their conduct this way as any other family whatsoever. The head of this branch is now in town, and has brought up with him his son and daughter, who are all the children he has, in order to be put some way into the world, and see fashions. They are both very ill-bred cubs; and having lived together from their infancy, without knowledge of the distinctions and decencies that are proper to be paid to each other's sex, they squabble like two brothers. The father is one of those who knows no better than that all pleasure is debauchery, and imagines, when he sees a man become his estate, that he will certainly spend it. This branch are a people who never had among them one man eminent either for good or ill: however, have all along kept their heads just above water, not by a prudent and regular economy, but by expedients in the matches they have made in to their house. When one of the family has in the pursuit of foxes, and in the entertainment of clowns, run out the third part of the value of his estate, such a spendthrift has dressed up his eldest son, and married what they call a good fortune: who has supported the father as a tyrant over them during his life, in the same house or neighbourhood. The son, in succession, has just taken the same method to keep up his dignity, till the mortgages he has ate and drank himself into have reduced him to the necessity of sacrificing his son also, in imitation of his progenitor. This had been for many generations, the whole that had happened in the family of Sam Bickerstaff, till the time of my present cousin Samuel, the father of the young people we have just now spoken of.

Samuel Bickerstaff, esquire, is so happy as that by several legacies from distant relations, deaths of maiden sisters, and other instances of good fortune, he has besides his real estate, a great sum of ready money. His son at the same time knows he has a good fortune, which the father cannot alienate; though he strives to make him believe he depends only on his will for maintenance. Tom is now in his nineteenth year. Mrs. Mary in her fifteenth. Cousin Samuel, who understands no one point of good behaviour as it regards all the rest of the world, is an exact critic in the dress, the motion, the looks, and gestures, of his children. What adds to their misery is, that he is excessively fond of them, and the greatest part of their time is spent in the presence of this nice observer. Their life is one of continued constraint. The girl never turns her head, but she is warned not to follow the proud minxes of the town. The boy is not to turn fop, or be quarrelsome, at the same time not to take an affront. I had the good fortune to dine with him to-day, and heard his fatherly table-talk as we sat at dinner, which, if my memory does not fail me, for the benefit of the world, I shall set down as he spoke it; which was much as follows, and may be of great use to those parents who seem to make it a rule, that their children's turn to enjoy the world is not to commence till they themselves have left it.

"Now, Tom, I have bought you chambers in the inns of court. I allow you to take a walk once or twice a day round the garden. If you mind your business, you need not study to be as great a lawyer as Coke upon Littleton. I have that that will keep you; but be sure you keep an exact account of your linen. Write down what you give out to your laundress, and what she brings home again. Go as little as possible to the other end of the town; but if you do, come home early. I believe I was as sharp as you for your years, and I had my hat snatched off my head coming home late at a stop by St. Clement's church, and I do not know from that day to this who took it. I do not care if you learn to fence a little; for I would not have you made a fool of. Let me have an account of everything, every post; I am willing to be at that charge, and I think you need not spare your pains. As for you, daughter Molly, do not mind one word that is said to you in London, for it is only for your money."

XVIII.—BICKERSTAFF CENSOR:—CASES IN COURT.

From my own Apartment, December 5.

There is nothing gives a man greater satisfaction than the sense of having despatched a great deal of business, especially when it turns to the public emolument. I have much pleasure of this kind upon my spirits at present, occasioned by the fatigue of affairs which I went through last Saturday. It is some time since I set apart that day for examining the pretensions of several who had applied to me for canes, perspective glasses, snuff-boxes, orange-flower-waters, and the like ornaments of life. In order to adjust this matter, I had before directed Charles Lillie of Beaufort Buildings to prepare a great bundle of blank licenses in the following words:

"You are hereby required to permit the bearer of this cane to pass and repass through the streets and suburbs of London, or any place within ten miles of it, without let or molestation, provided that he does not walk with it under his arm, brandish it in the air, or hang it on a button: in which case it shall be forfeited; and I hereby declare it forfeited, to any one who shall think it safe to take it from him.
    "*Isaac Bickerstaff.*"

The same form, differing only in the provisos, will serve for a perspective, snuff-box, or perfumed handkerchief. I had placed myself in my elbow-chair at the upper end of my great parlour, having ordered Charles Lillie to take his place upon a joint stool, with a writing-desk before him. John Morphew also took his station at the door; I having, for his good and faithful services, appointed him my chamber-keeper upon court days. He let me know that there were a great number attending without. Upon which I ordered him to give notice, that I did not intend to sit upon snuff-boxes that day; but that those who appeared for canes might enter. The first presented me with the following petition, which I ordered Mr. Lillie to read.

"*To Isaac Bickerstaff, esquire, censor of great Britain.*

"The humble petition of *Simon* TRIPPIT,

"Showeth,

"That your petitioner having been bred up to a cane from his youth, it is now become as necessary to him as any other of his limbs.

"That, a great part of his behaviour depending upon it, he should be reduced to the utmost necessities if he should lose the use of it.

"That the knocking of it upon his shoe, leaning one leg upon it, or whistling with it on his mouth, are such great reliefs to him in conversation, that he does not know how to be good company without it.

"That he is at present engaged in an amour, and must despair of success if it be taken from him.

"Your petitioner, therefore, hopes, that the premises tenderly considered, your Worship will not deprive him of so useful and so necessary a support.

"And your petitioner shall ever, *etc.*"

Upon the hearing of his case, I was touched with some compassion, and the more so, when, upon observing him nearer, I found he was a prig. I bade him produce his cane in court, which he had left at the door. He did so, and I finding it to be very curiously clouded with a transparent amber head, and a blue riband to hang upon his wrist, I immediately ordered my clerk Lillie to lay it up, and deliver out to him a plain joint headed with walnut; and then, in order to wean him from it by degrees, permitted him to wear it three days in a week, and to abate proportionably till he found himself able to go alone.

The second who appeared came limping into the court; and setting forth in his petition many pretences for the use of a cane, I caused them to be examined one by one, but finding him in different stories, and confronting him with several witnesses who had seen him walk upright, I ordered Mr. Lillie to take in his cane, and rejected his petition as frivolous.

A third made his entry with great difficulty, leaning upon a slight stick, and in danger of falling every step he took. I saw the weakness of his hams; and I bade him leave his cane, and gave him a new pair of crutches, with which he went off in great vigour and alacrity. This gentleman was succeeded by another, who seemed very much pleased while his petition was reading, in which he had represented, That he was extremely afflicted with the gout, and set his foot upon the ground with the caution and dignity which accompany that distemper. I suspected him for an impostor, and, having ordered him to be searched, I committed him into the hands of Doctor Thomas Smith in King Street, my own corn-cutter, who attended in an outward room: and wrought so speedy a cure upon him, that I thought fit to send him also away without his cane.

While I was thus dispensing justice, I heard a noise in my outward room; and inquiring what was the occasion of it, my door-keeper told me, that they had taken one up in the very fact as he was passing by my door. They immediately brought in a lively fresh-coloured young man, who made great resistance with hand and foot, but did not offer to make use of his cane, which hung upon his fifth button. Upon examination, I found him to be an Oxford scholar who was just entered at the Temple. He at first disputed the jurisdiction of the court; but, being driven out of his little law and logic, he told me very pertly, "that he looked upon such a perpendicular creature as man to make a very imperfect figure without a cane in his hand. It is well known," says he, "we ought, according to the natural situation of our bodies, to walk upon our hands and feet: and that the wisdom of the ancients had described man to be an animal of four legs in the morning, two at noon, and three at night; by which they intimated that a cane might very properly become part of us in some period of life." Upon which I asked him, whether he wore it at his breast to have it in readiness when that period should arrive. My young lawyer immediately told me, he had a property in it, and a right to hang it where he pleased, and to make use of it as he thought fit, provided that he did not break the peace with it; and farther said, that he never took it off his button, unless it were to lift it up at a coachman, hold it over the head of a drawer, point out the circumstances of a story, or for other services of the like nature, that are all within the laws of the land. I did not care for discouraging a young man, who, I saw, would come to good; and, because his heart was set upon his new purchase, I only ordered him to wear it about his neck, instead of hanging it upon his button, and so dismissed him.

There were several appeared in court, whose pretensions I found to be very good, and, therefore, gave them their licenses upon paying their fees; as many others had their licenses renewed, who required more time for recovery of their lameness than I had before allowed them.

Having despatched this set of my petitioners, there came in a well-dressed man with a glass tube in one hand, and his petition in the other. Upon his entering the room, he threw back the right side of his wig, put forward his right leg, and advancing the glass to his right eye, aimed it directly at me. In the meanwhile, to make my observations also, I put on my spectacles, in which posture we surveyed each other for some time. Upon the removal of our glasses I desired him to read his petition, which he did very promptly and easily; though at the same time it set forth that he could see nothing distinctly, and was within very few degrees of being utterly blind, concluding with a prayer that he might be permitted to strengthen and extend his sight by a glass. In answer to this I told him he might sometimes extend it to his own destruction. "As you are now," said I, "you are out of the reach of beauty, the shafts of the finest eyes lose their force before they can come at you; you cannot distinguish a Toast from an orange-wench; you can see a whole circle of beauty without any interruption from an impertinent face to discompose you. In short, what are snares for others—" My petitioner would hear no more, but told me very seriously, "Mr. Bickerstaff, you quite mistake your man; it is the joy, the pleasure, the employment, of my life to frequent public assemblies, and gaze upon the fair." In a word, I found his use of a glass was occasioned by no other infirmity than his vanity, and was not so much designed to make him see, as to make him be seen and distinguished by others. I therefore refused him a license for a perspective, but allowed him a pair of spectacles, with full permission to use them in any public assembly as he should think fit. He was followed by so very few of this order of men that I have reason to hope this sort of cheats are almost at an end.

The orange-flower-men appeared next with petitions perfumed so strongly with musk, that I was almost overcome with the scent; and for my own sake was obliged forthwith to license their handkerchiefs, especially when I found they had sweetened them at Charles Lillie's, and that some of their persons would not be altogether inoffensive without them. John Morphew, whom I have made the general of my dead men, acquainted me that the petitioners were all of that order, and could produce certificates to prove it if I required it. I was so well pleased with this way of embalming themselves that I commanded the above-said Morphew to give it in his orders to his whole army, that every one, who did not surrender himself to be disposed of by the upholders, should use the same method to keep himself sweet during his present state of putrefaction.

I finished my session with great content of mind, reflecting upon the good I had done; for, however slightly men may regard these particularities, "and little follies in dress and behaviour, they lead to greater evils. The bearing to be laughed at for such singularities, teaches us insensibly an impertinent fortitude, and enables us to bear public censure for things which more substantially deserve it." By this means they open a gate to folly, and oftentimes render a man so ridiculous, as discredit his virtues and capacities, and unqualify them from doing any good in the world. Besides, the giving into uncommon habits of this nature is a want of that humble deference which is due to mankind, and, what is worst of all, the certain indication of some secret flaw in the mind of the person that commits them. When I was a young man, I remember a gentleman of great integrity and worth, was very remarkable for wearing a broad belt, and a hanger instead of a fashionable sword, though in all other points a very well-bred man. I suspected him at first sight to have something wrong in him, but was not able for a long time to discover any collateral proofs of it. I watched him narrowly for six-and-thirty years, when at last, to the surprise of everybody but myself, who had long expected to see the folly break out, he married his own cook-maid.

- - - - -

Sheer Lane, December 21.

As soon as I had placed myself in my chair of judicature, I ordered my clerk, Mr. Lillie, to read to the assembly, who were gathered together according to notice, a certain declaration, by way of charge, to open the purpose of my session, which tended only to this explanation, that as other courts were often called to demand the execution of persons dead in law; so this was held to give the last orders relating to those who are dead in reason. The solicitor of the new Company of Upholders, near the Haymarket, appeared in behalf of that useful society, and brought in an accusation of a young woman, who herself stood at the bar before me. Mr. Lillie read her indictment, which was in substance, "That, whereas Mrs. Rebecca Pindust, of the parish of Saint Martin-in-the-Fields, had, by the use of one instrument called a looking-glass, and by the further use of certain attire, made either of cambric, muslin, or other linen wares, upon her head, attained to such an evil art and magical force in the motion of her eyes and turn of her countenance, that she the said Rebecca had put to death several young men of the said parish; and that the said young men had acknowledged in certain papers, commonly called love-letters, which were produced in court, gilded on the edges, and sealed *with* A *particular wax*, with certain amorous and enchanting words wrought upon the said seals, that they died for the said Rebecca: and, whereas the said Rebecca persisted in the said evil practice; this way of life the said society construed to be, according to former edicts, a state of death, and demanded an order for the interment of the said Rebecca."

I looked upon the maid with great humanity, and desired her to make answer to what was said against her. She said, "It was indeed true, that she had practised all the arts and means she could, to dispose of herself happily in marriage, but thought she did not come under the censure expressed in my writings for the same; and humbly hoped I would not condemn her for the ignorance of her accusers, who, according to their own words, had rather represented her killing than dead." She further alleged, "That the expressions mentioned in the papers written to her were become mere words, and that she had been always ready to marry any of those who said they died for her; but that they made their escape, as soon as they found themselves pitied or believed." She ended her discourse by desiring I would for the future settle the meaning of the words "I die," in letters of love.

Mrs. Pindust behaved herself with such an air of innocence, that she easily gained credit, and was acquitted. Upon which occasion I gave it as a standing rule, "That any person, who in any letter, billet, or discourse, should tell a woman he died for her, should, if she pleased, be obliged to live with her, or be immediately interred upon such their own confessions without bail or mainprize."

It happened that the very next who was brought before me was one of her admirers, who was indicted upon that very head. A letter, which he acknowledged to be his own hand, was read, in which were the following words, "Cruel creature, I die for you." It was observable that he took snuff all the time his accusation was reading. I asked him, "how he came to use these words, if he were not a dead man?" He told me, "he was in love with the lady, and did not know any other way of telling her so; and that all his acquaintance took the same method." Though I was moved with compassion towards him, by reason of the weakness of his parts, yet for example sake I was forced to answer, "Your sentence shall be a warning to all the rest of your companions, not to tell lies for want of wit." Upon this, he began to beat his snuff-box with a very saucy air; and opening it again, "Faith, Isaac," said he, "thou art a very unaccountable old fellow—Pr'ythee, who gave thee the power of life and death? What hast thou to do with ladies and lovers? I suppose thou wouldst have a man be in company with his mistress, and say nothing to her. Dost thou call breaking a jest telling a lie? Ha! is that thy wisdom, old stiffback, ha?" He was going on with this insipid commonplace mirth, sometimes opening his box, sometimes shutting it, then viewing the picture on the lid, and then the workmanship of the hinge, when, in the midst of his eloquence, I ordered his box to be taken from him; upon which he was immediately struck speechless, and carried off stone dead.

The next who appeared was a hale old fellow of sixty. He was brought in by his relations, who desired leave to bury him. Upon requiring a distinct account of the prisoner, a credible witness deposed, "that he always rose at ten of the clock, played with his cat till twelve, smoked tobacco till one, was at dinner till two, then took another pipe, played at backgammon till six, talked of one Madame Frances, an old mistress of his, till eight, repeated the same account at the tavern till ten, then returned home, took the other pipe, and then to bed." I asked him, "what he had to say for himself?"—"As to what," said he, "they mention concerning Madame Frances—"

I did not care for hearing a Canterbury tale, and, therefore, thought myself seasonably interrupted by a young gentleman, who appeared in the behalf of the old man, and prayed an arrest of judgment; "for that he, the said young man, held certain lands by his the said old man's life." Upon this, the solicitor of the Upholders took an occasion to demand him also, and thereupon produced several evidences that witnessed to his life and conversation. It appeared that each of them divided their hours in matters of equal moment and importance to themselves and to the public. They rose at the same hour: while the old man was playing with his cat, the young one was looking out of his window; while the old man was smoking his pipe, the young man was rubbing his teeth; while one was at dinner, the other was dressing; while one was at backgammon, the other was at dinner; while the old fellow was talking of Madame Frances, the young one was either at play, or toasting women whom he never conversed with. The only difference was, that the young man had never been good for anything; the old man a man of worth before he know Madame Frances. Upon the whole, I ordered them to be both interred together, with inscriptions proper to their characters, signifying, that the old man died in the year 1689, and was buried in the year 1709; and over the young one it was said, that he departed this world in the twenty-fifth year of his death.

The next class of criminals were authors in prose and verse. Those of them who had produced any stillborn work were immediately dismissed to their burial, and were followed by others, who notwithstanding some sprightly issue in their lifetime, had given proofs of their death, by some posthumous children, that bore no resemblance to their elder brethren. As for those who were the fathers of a mixed progeny, provided always they could prove the last to be a live child, they escaped with life, but not without loss of limbs; for, in this case, I was satisfied with amputation of the parts which were mortified.

These were followed by a great crowd of superannuated benchers of the Inns of Court, senior fellows of colleges, and defunct statesmen: all whom I ordered to be decimated indifferently, allowing the rest a reprieve for one year, with a promise of a free pardon in case of resuscitation.

There were still great multitudes to be examined; but, finding it very late, I adjourned the court, not without the secret pleasure that I had done my duty, and furnished out a handsome execution.

- - - - -

Haymarket, December 23.

Whereas the gentleman that behaved himself in a very disobedient and obstinate manner at his late trial in Sheer Lane on the twentieth instant, and was carried off

60

dead upon taking away of his snuff-box, remains still unburied; the company of Upholders, not knowing otherwise how they should be paid, have taken his goods in execution to defray the charge of his funeral. His said effects are to be exposed to sale by auction, at their office in the Haymarket, on the fourth of January next, and are as follow:—

A very rich tweezer-case, containing twelve instruments for the use of each hour in the day.

Four pounds of scented snuff, with three gilt snuff-boxes; one of them with an invisible hinge, and a looking-glass in the lid.

Two more of ivory, with the portraitures on their lids of two ladies of the town; the originals to be seen every night in the side-boxes of the playhouse.

A sword with a steel diamond hilt, never drawn but once at May-fair.

Six clean packs of cards, a quart of orange-flower-water, a pair of French scissors, a toothpick-case, and an eyebrow brush.

A large glass-case, containing the linen and clothes of the deceased; among which are, two embroidered suits, a pocket perspective, a dozen pair of *red-heeled shoes*, three pair of *red silk stockings*, and an amber-headed cane.

The strong box of the deceased, wherein were found five billet-doux, a Bath shilling, a crooked sixpence, a silk garter, a lock of hair, and three broken fans.

A press for books; containing on the upper shelf—

Three bottles of diet-drink.
Two boxes of pills.
A syringe, and other mathematical instruments.

On the second shelf are several miscellaneous works, as

Lampoons.
Plays.
Tailors' bills.
And an almanack for the year seventeen hundred.

On the third shelf—

A bundle of letters unopened, indorsed, in the hand of the deceased, "Letters from the old Gentleman."
Lessons for the flute.

Toland's "Christianity not mysterious;" and a paper filled with patterns of several fashionable stuffs.

On the lowest shelf—

One shoe.
A pair of snuffers.
A French grammar.
A mourning hat-band; and half a bottle of usquebaugh.

There will be added to these goods, to make a complete auction, a collection of gold snuff-boxes and clouded canes, which are to continue in fashion for three months after the sale.

The whole are to be set up and prized by Charles Bubbleboy, who is to open the auction with a speech.

I find I am so very unhappy, that, while I am busy in correcting the folly and vice of one sex, several exorbitances break out in the other. I have not thoroughly examined their new fashioned petticoats, but shall set aside one day in the next week for that purpose. The following petition on this subject was presented to me this morning:—

"The humble petition of William Jingle, Coach-maker and Chair-maker, of the Liberty of Westminster:

"*To Isaac Bickerstaff, esquire, censor of great Britain*:

"Showeth,

"That upon the late invention of Mrs. Catharine Cross-stitch, mantua-maker, the petticoats of ladies were too wide for entering into any coach or chair, which was in use before the said invention.

"That for the service of the said ladies, your petitioner has built a round chair, in the form of a lantern, six yards and a half in circumference, with a stool in the centre of it: the said vehicle being so contrived, as to receive the passenger by opening in two in the middle, and closing mathematically when she is seated.

"That your petitioner has also invented a coach for the reception of one lady only, who is to be let in at the top.

"That the said coach has been tried by a lady's woman in one of these full petticoats, who was let down from a balcony, and drawn up again by pulleys, to the great satisfaction of her lady, and all who behold her.

"Your petitioner, therefore, most humbly prays, that for the encouragement of ingenuity and useful inventions, he may be heard before you pass sentence upon the petticoats aforesaid.

"And your petitioner," *etc.*

I have likewise received a female petition, signed by several thousands, praying that I would not any longer defer giving judgment in the case of the petticoat, many of them having put off the making new clothes, till such time as they know what verdict will pass upon it. I do, therefore, hereby certify to all whom it may concern, that I do design to set apart Tuesday next for the final determination of that matter, having already ordered a jury of matrons to be impannelled, for the clearing up of any difficult points that may arise in the trial.

- - - - -

keep out of the way and abscond, for fear of being buried; and being willing to respite their interment, in consideration of their families, and in hopes of their amendment, I shall allow them certain privileged places, where they may appear to one another, without causing any let or molestation to the living, or receiving any, in their own persons, from the company of Upholders. Between the hours of seven and nine in the morning, they may appear in safety at Saint James's coffee-house, or at White's, if they do not keep their beds, which is more proper for men in their condition. From nine to eleven I allow them to walk from Story's to Rosamond's pond in the Park or in any other public walks which are not frequented by the living at that time. Between eleven and three they are to vanish, and keep out of sight till three in the afternoon, at which time they may go to 'Change till five; and then, if they please, divert themselves at the Haymarket, or Drury Lane until the play begins. It is further granted in favour of these persons, that they may be received at any table, where there are more present than seven in number: provided that they do not take upon them to talk, judge, commend, or find fault with any speech, action, or behaviour of the living. In which case it shall be lawful to seize their persons at any place or hour whatsoever, and to convey their bodies to the next undertaker's; anything in this advertisement to the contrary notwithstanding.

- - - - -

Sheer Lane, January 4.

The court being prepared for proceeding on the cause of the petticoat, I gave orders to bring in a criminal, who was taken up as she went out of the puppet-show about three nights ago, and was now standing in the street, with a great concourse of people about her. Word was brought me that she had endeavoured twice or thrice to come in, but could not do it by reason of her petticoat, which was too large for the entrance of my house, though I had ordered both the folding-doors to be thrown open for its reception. Upon this, I desired the jury of matrons, who stood at my right hand, to inform themselves whether there were any private reasons why she might not make her appearance separate from her petticoat. This was managed with great discretion, and had such an effect, that upon the return of the verdict from the bench of matrons, I issued out an order forthwith, "that the criminal should be stripped of her encumbrances till she became little enough to enter my house." I had before given directions for an engine of several legs that could contract or open itself like the top of an umbrella, in order to place the petticoat upon it, by which means I might take a leisurely survey of it, as it should appear in its proper dimensions. This was all done accordingly; and forthwith, upon the closing of the engine, the petticoat was brought into court. I then directed the machine to be set upon the table and dilated in such a manner as to show the garment in its utmost circumference; but my great hall was too narrow for the experiment; for before it was half unfolded, it described so immoderate a circle, that the lower part of it brushed upon my face as I sat in my chair of judicature. I then inquired for the person that belonged to the petticoat; and to my great surprise, was directed to a very beautiful young damsel, with so pretty a face and shape, that I bid her come out of the crowd, and seated her upon a little crock at my left hand. "My pretty maid," said I, "do you own yourself to have been the inhabitant of the garment before us?" The girl, I found, had good sense, and told me with a smile, that, "notwithstanding it was her own petticoat, she should be very glad to see an example made of it; and that she wore it for no other reason, but that she had a mind to look as big and burly as other persons of her quality; that she had kept out of it as long as she could, and till she began to appear little in the eyes of her acquaintance; that, if she laid it aside, people would think she was not made like other women." I always give great allowances to the fair sex upon account of the fashion, and, therefore, was not displeased with the defence of the pretty criminal. I then ordered the vest which stood before us to be drawn up by a pulley to the top of my great hall, and afterwards to be spread open by the engine it was placed upon, in such a manner, that it formed a very splendid and ample canopy over our heads, and covered the whole court of judicature with a kind of silken rotunda, in its form not unlike the cupola of St. Paul's. I entered upon the whole cause with great satisfaction as I sat under the shadow of it.

The counsel for the petticoat were now called in, and ordered to produce what they had to say against the popular cry which was raised against it. They answered the objections with great strength and solidity of argument, and expatiated in very florid harangues, which they did not fail to set off and furbelow, if I may be allowed the metaphor, with many periodical sentences and turns of oratory. The chief arguments for their client were taken, first, from the great benefit that might arise to our woollen manufactory from this invention, which was calculated as follows. The common petticoat has not above four yards in the circumference; whereas this over our heads had more in the semi-diameter; so that, by allowing it twenty-four yards in the circumference, the five millions of woollen petticoats, which, according to Sir William Petty, supposing what ought to be supposed in a well-governed state, that all petticoats are made of that stuff, would amount to thirty millions of those of the ancient mode: a prodigious improvement of the woollen trade! and what could not fail to sink the power of France in a few years.

To introduce the second argument, they begged leave to read a petition of the ropemakers, wherein it was represented, "that the demand for cords, and the price of them, were much risen since this fashion came up." At this, all the company who were present lifted up their eyes into the vault; and I must confess, we did discover many traces of cordage, which were interwoven in the stiffening of the drapery.

A third argument was founded upon a petition of the Greenland trade, which likewise represented the great consumption of whalebone which would be occasioned by the present fashion, and the benefit which would thereby accrue to that branch of the British trade.

To conclude, they gently touched upon the weight and unwieldiness of the garment, which they insinuated might be of great use.

These arguments would have wrought very much upon me, as I then told the company in a long and elaborate discourse, had I not considered the great and additional expense which such fashions would bring upon fathers and husbands; and, therefore, by no means to be thought of till some years after a peace. I further urged, that it would be a prejudice to the ladies themselves, who could never expect to have any money in the pocket if they laid out so much on the petticoat.

At the same time, in answer to the several petitions produced on that side, I showed one subscribed by the women of several persons of quality, humbly setting forth, "that, since the introduction of this mode, their respective ladies had, instead of bestowing on them their cast gowns, cut them into shreds, and mixed them with the cordage and buckram, to complete the stiffening of their under petticoats." For which, and sundry other reasons, I pronounced the petticoat a forfeiture; but to show that I did not make that judgment for the sake of filthy lucre, I ordered it to be folded up, and sent it as a present to a widow-gentlewoman who has five daughters, desiring she would make each of them a petticoat out of it, and send me back the remainder, which I design to cut into stomachers, caps, facings of my waistcoat-sleeves, and other garnitures suitable to my age and quality.

I would not be understood that, while I discard this monstrous invention, I am an enemy to the proper ornaments of the fair sex. On the contrary, as the hand of nature has poured on them such a profusion of charms and graces, and sent them into the world more amiable and finished than the rest of her works; so I would have them bestow upon themselves all the additional beauties that art can supply them with; provided it does not interfere with disguise, or pervert those of nature.

I consider woman as a beautiful romantic animal, that may be adorned with furs and feathers, pearls and diamonds, ores and silks. The lynx shall cast its skin at her feet to make her a tippet; the peacock, parrot, and swan shall pay contributions to her muff; the sea shall be searched for shells, and the rocks for gems; and every part of nature furnish out its share towards the embellishment of a creature that is the most consummate work of it. All this I shall indulge them in; but as for the petticoat I have been speaking of, I neither can nor will allow it.

XIX.—OF MEN WHO ARE NOT THEIR OWN MASTERS.

From my own Apartment, June 2.

I have received a letter which accuses me of partiality in the administration of the censorship; and says, that I have been very free with the lower part of mankind, but extremely cautious in representations of matters which concern men of condition. This correspondent takes upon him also to say, the upholsterer was not undone by turning politician, but became bankrupt by trusting his goods to persons of quality; and demands of me, that I should do justice upon such as brought poverty and distress upon the world below them, while they themselves were sunk in pleasures and luxury, supported at the expense of those very persons whom they treated with a negligence, as if they did not know whether they dealt with them or not. This is a very heavy accusation, both of me and such as the man aggrieved accuses me of tolerating. For this reason, I resolved to take this matter into consideration; and, upon very little meditation, could call to my memory many instances which made this complaint far from being groundless. The root of this evil does not always proceed from injustice in the men of figure, but often from a false grandeur which they take upon them in being unacquainted with their own business; not considering how mean a part they act when their names and characters are subjected to the little arts of their servants and dependants. The overseers of the poor are a people who have no great reputation for the discharge of their trust, but are much less scandalous than the overseers of the rich. Ask a young fellow of a great estate, who was that odd fellow that spoke to him in a public place? he answers, "one that does my business." It is, with many, a natural consequence of being a man of fortune, that they are not to understand the disposal of it; and they long to come to their estates, only to put themselves under new guardianship. Nay, I have known a young fellow, who was regularly bred an attorney, and was a very expert one till he had an estate fallen to him. The moment that happened, he, who could before prove the next land he cast his eye upon his own; and was so sharp, that a man at first sight would give him a small sum for a general receipt, whether he owed him anything or not: such a one, I say, have I seen, upon coming to an estate, forget all his diffidence of mankind, and become the most manageable thing breathing. He immediately wanted a stirring man to take upon him his affairs; to receive and pay, and do everything which he himself was now too fine a gentleman to understand. It is pleasant to consider, that he who would have got an estate, had he not come to one, will certainly starve because one fell to him; but such contradictions are we to ourselves, and any change of life is insupportable to some natures.

It is a mistaken sense of superiority to believe a figure, or equipage, gives men precedence to their neighbours. Nothing can create respect from mankind, but laying obligations upon them; and it may very reasonably be concluded, that if it were put into a due balance, according to the true state of the account, many who believe themselves in possession of a large share of dignity in the world, must give place to their inferiors. The greatest of all distinctions in civil life is that of debtor and creditor; and there needs no great progress in logic to know which, in that case, is the advantageous side. He who can say to another, "Pray, master," or "pray, my lord, give me my own," can as justly tell him, "It is a fantastical distinction you take upon you, to pretend to pass upon the world for my master or lord, when, at the same time that I wear your livery, you owe me wages; or, while I wait at your door, you are ashamed to see me till you have paid my bill."

The good old way among the gentry of England to maintain their pre-eminence over the lower rank, was by their bounty, munificence, and hospitality; and it is a very unhappy change, if at present, by themselves or their agents, the luxury of the gentry is supported by the credit of the trader. This is what my correspondent pretends to prove out of his own books, and those of his whole neighbourhood. He has the confidence to say, that there is a mug-house near Long Acre, where you may every evening hear an exact account of distresses of this kind. One complains that such a lady's finery is the occasion that his own wife and daughter appear so long in the same gown. Another, that all the furniture of her visiting apartment are no more hers than the scenery of a play are the proper goods of the actress. Nay, at the lower end of the same table, you may hear a butcher and a poulterer say, that, at their proper charge, all that family has been maintained since they last came to town.

The free manner in which people of fashion are discoursed on at such meetings is but a just reproach for their failures in this kind; but the melancholy relations of the great necessities tradesmen are driven to, who support their credit in spite of the faithless promises which are made them, and the abatement which they suffer when paid by the extortion of upper servants, is what would stop the most thoughtless man in the career of his pleasures, if rightly represented to him.

If this matter be not very speedily amended, I shall think fit to print exact lists of all persons who are not at their own disposal, though above the age of twenty-one; and as the trader is made bankrupt for absence from his abode, so shall the gentleman for being at home, if, when Mr. Morphew calls, he cannot give him an exact account of what passes in his own family. After this fair warning, no one ought to think himself hardly dealt with, if I take upon me to pronounce him no longer master of his estate, wife, or family, than he continues to improve, cherish, and maintain them upon the basis of his own property, without incursions upon his neighbour in any of these particulars.

According to that excellent philosopher Epictetus, we are all but acting parts in a play; and it is not a distinction in itself to be high or low, but to become the parts we are to perform. I am, by my office, prompter on this occasion, and shall give those who are a little out in their parts such soft hints as may help them to proceed, without letting it be known to the audience they were out; but if they run quite out of character, they must be called off the stage, and receive parts more suitable to their genius. Servile complaisance shall degrade a man from his honour and quality, and haughtiness be yet more debased. Fortune shall no longer appropriate distinctions, but nature direct us in the disposition both of respect and discountenance. As there are tempers made for command and others for obedience, so there are men born for acquiring possessions, and others incapable of being other than mere lodgers in the houses of their ancestors, and have it not in their very composition to be proprietors of anything. These men are moved only by the mere effects of impulse: their good-will and disesteem are to be regarded equally, for neither is the effect of their judgment. This loose temper is that which makes a man, what Sallust so well remarks to happen frequently in the same person, to be covetous of what is another's, and profuse of what is his own. This sort of men is usually amiable to ordinary eyes; but, in the sight of reason, nothing is laudable but what is guided by reason. The covetous prodigal is of all others the worst man in society. If he would but take time to look into himself, he would find his soul all over gashed with broken vows and promises; and his retrospect on his actions would not consist of reflections upon those good resolutions after mature thought, which are the true life of a reasonable creature, but the nauseous memory of imperfect pleasures, idle dreams, and occasional amusements. To follow such dissatisfying pursuits is it possible to suffer the ignominy of being unjust? I remember in Tully's Epistle, in the recommendation of a man to an affair which had no manner of relation to money, it is said, "You may trust him, for he is a frugal man." It is certain, he who has not a regard to strict justice in the commerce of life, can be capable of no good action in any other kind; but he who lives below his income, lays up every moment of life armour against a base world, that will cover all his frailties while he is so fortified, and exaggerate them when he is naked and defenceless.

ADVERTISEMENT.

to Mr. Tiptoe's dancing-school, and returns at eleven every evening, for one shilling and four-pence.

N.B.—Dancing shoes, not exceeding four inches height in the heel, and periwigs, not exceeding three feet in length, are carried in the coach-box gratis.

XX.—FALSE DOCTORING.

From my own Apartment, October 2O.

I do not remember that in any of my lucubrations I have touched upon that useful science of physic, notwithstanding I have declared myself more than once a professor of it. I have indeed joined the study of astrology with it, because I never knew a physician recommend himself to the public who had not a sister art to embellish his knowledge in medicine. It has been commonly observed, in compliment to the ingenious of our profession, that Apollo was god of verse as well as physic; and in all ages, the most celebrated practitioners of our country were the particular favourites of the Muses. Poetry to physic is indeed like the gilding to a pill; it makes the art shine, and covers the severity of the doctor with the agreeableness of the companion.

The very foundation of poetry is good sense, if we may allow Horace to be a judge of the art.

"Scribendi recte sapere est et principium et fons."
Hor. ARS *poet.* 3O9.

"Such judgment is the ground of writing well."
Roscommon.

And if so, we have reason to believe that the same man who writes well can prescribe well, if he has applied himself to the study of both. Besides, when we see a man making profession of two different sciences, it is natural for us to believe he is no pretender in that which we are not judges of, when we find him skilful in that which we understand.

Ordinary quacks and charlatans are thoroughly sensible how necessary it is to support themselves by these collateral assistances, and therefore always lay their claim to some supernumerary accomplishments, which are wholly foreign to their profession.

About twenty years ago, it was impossible to walk the streets without having an advertisement thrust into your hand, of a doctor "who was arrived at the knowledge of the 'Green and Red Dragon,' and had discovered the female fern-seed." Nobody ever knew what this meant; but the "Green and Red Dragon" so amused the people, that the doctor lived very comfortably upon them. About the same time there was pasted a very hard word upon every corner of the streets. This, to the best of my remembrance, was

TETRACHYMAGOGON,

which drew great shoals of spectators about it, who read the bill that it introduced with unspeakable curiosity; and when they were sick, would have nobody but this learned man for their physician.

I once received an advertisement of one "who had studied thirty years by candle-light for the good of his countrymen." He might have studied twice as long by daylight and never have been taken notice of. But elucubrations cannot be over-valued. There are some who have gained themselves great reputation for physic by their birth, as the "seventh son of a seventh son," and others by not being born at all, as the unborn doctor, who I hear is lately gone the way of his patients, having died worth five hundred pounds per annum, though he was not born to a halfpenny.

My ingenious friend, Doctor Saffold, succeeded my old contemporary, Doctor Lilly, in the studies both of physic and astrology, to which he added that of poetry, as was to be seen both upon the sign where he lived, and in the pills which he distributed. He was succeeded by Doctor Case, who erased the verses of his predecessor out of the sign-post, and substituted in their stead two of his own, which were as follow:—

"Within this place
Lives Doctor Case."

He is said to have got more by this distich than Mr. Dryden did by all his works. There would be no end of enumerating the several imaginary perfections and unaccountable artifices by which this tribe of men ensnare the minds of the vulgar and gain crowds of admirers. I have seen the whole front of a mountebank's stage from one end to the other, faced with patents, certificates, medals, and great seals, by which the several princes of Europe have testified their particular respect and esteem for the doctor. Every great man with a sounding title has been his patient. I believe I have seen twenty mountebanks that have given physic to the Czar of Muscovy. The Great Duke of Tuscany escapes no better. The Elector of Brandenburg was likewise a very good patient.

This great condescension of the doctor draws upon him much good-will from his audience; and it is ten to one but if any of them be troubled with an aching tooth, his ambition will prompt him to get it drawn by a person who has had so many princes, kings, and emperors under his hands.

I must not leave this subject without observing that, as physicians are apt to deal in poetry, apothecaries endeavour to recommend themselves by oratory, and are therefore, without controversy, the most eloquent persons in the whole British nation. I would not willingly discourage any of the arts, especially that of which I am an humble professor; but I must confess, for the good of my native country, I could wish there might be a suspension of physic for some years, that our kingdom, which has been so much exhausted by the wars, might have leave to recruit itself.

As for myself, the only physic which has brought me safe to almost the age of man, and which I prescribe to all my friends, is Abstinence. This is certainly the best physic for prevention, and very often the most effectual against a present distemper. In short, my recipe is "Take nothing."

Were the body politic to be physicked like particular persons, I should venture to prescribe to it after the same manner. I remember when our whole island was shaken with an earthquake some years ago, there was an impudent mountebank who sold pills, which, as he told the country people, were "very good against an earthquake." It may, perhaps, be thought as absurd to prescribe a diet for the allaying popular commotions and national ferments. But I am verily persuaded that if in such a case a whole people were to enter into a course of abstinence, and eat nothing but water-gruel for a fortnight, it would abate the rage and animosity of parties, and not a little contribute to the care of a distracted nation. Such a fast would have a natural tendency to the procuring of those ends, for which a fast is usually proclaimed. If any man has a mind to enter on such a voluntary abstinence, it might not be improper to give him the caution of Pythagoras in particular, Abstine a fabis, "Abstain from beans," that is, say the interpreters, "Meddle not with elections," beans having been made use of by the voters among the Athenians in the choice of magistrates.

XXI.—DRINKING.

From my own Apartment, October 23.

A method of spending one's time agreeably is a thing so little studied, that the common amusement of our young gentlemen, especially of such as are at a distance from those of the first breeding, is Drinking. This way of entertainment has custom on its side; but as much as it has prevailed, I believe there have been very few companies that have been guilty of excess this way, where there have not happened more accidents which make against than for the continuance of it. It is very common that events arise from a debauch which are fatal, and always such as are disagreeable. With all a man's reason and good sense about him, his tongue is apt to utter things out of mere gaiety of heart, which may displease his best friends. Who then would trust himself to the power of wine without saying more against it, than that it raises the imagination and depresses the judgment? Were there only this single consideration, that we are less masters of ourselves when we drink in the least proportion above the exigencies of thirst, I say, were this all that could be objected, it were sufficient to make us abhor this vice. But we may go on to say, that as he who drinks but a little is not master of himself, so he who drinks much is a slave to himself. As for my part, I ever esteemed a drunkard of all vicious persons the most vicious: for if our actions are to be weighed and considered according to the intention of them, what cannot we think of him, who puts himself into a circumstance wherein he can have no intention at all, but incapacitates himself for the duties and offices of life by a suspension of all his faculties? If a man considered that he cannot, under the oppression of drink, be a friend, a gentleman, a master, or a subject: that he has so long banished himself from all that is dear, and given up all that is sacred to him: he would even then think of a debauch with horror. But when he looks still further and acknowledges that he is not only expelled out of all the relations of life, but also liable to offend against them all; what words can express the terror and detestation he would have of such a condition? And yet he owns all this of himself who says he was drunk last night.

As I have all along persisted in it, that all the vicious in general are in a state of death; so I think I may add to the non-existence of drunkards, that they died by their own hands. He is certainly as guilty of suicide who perishes by a slow, as he that is despatched by an immediate, poison. In my last lucubration I proposed the general use of water gruel, and hinted that it might not be amiss at this very season. But as there are some whose cases, in regard to their families, will not admit of delay, I have used my interest in several wards of the city, that the wholesome restorative above-mentioned may be given in tavern kitchens to all the morning draughtsmen within the walls when they call for wine before noon. For a further restraint and mark upon such persons, I have given orders, that in all the offices where policies are drawn upon lives, it shall be added to the article which prohibits that the nominee should cross the sea, the words, "Provided also, that the above-mentioned A. B. shall not drink before dinner during the term mentioned in this indenture."

I am not without hopes, that by this method I shall bring some unsizable friends of mine into shape and breadth, as well as others, who are languid and consumptive, into health and vigour. Most of the self-murderers whom I yet hinted at are such as preserve a certain regularity in taking their poison, and make it mix pretty well with their food. But the most conspicuous of those who destroy themselves, are such as in their youth fall into this sort of debauchery; and contract a certain uneasiness of spirit, which is not to be diverted but by tippling as often as they can fall into company in the day, and conclude with downright drunkenness at night. These gentlemen never know the satisfaction of youth, but skip the years of manhood, and are decrepit soon after they are of age. I was godfather to one of these old fellows. He is now three-and-thirty, which is the grand climacteric of a young drunkard. I went to visit the wretch this morning, with no other purpose but to rally him under the pain and uneasiness of being sober.

But as our faults are double when they affect others besides ourselves, so this vice is still more odious in a married than a single man. He that is the husband of a woman of honour, and comes home overloaded with wine, is still more contemptible in proportion to the regard we have to the unhappy consort of his bestiality. The imagination cannot shape to itself anything more monstrous and unnatural than the familiarities between drunkenness and chastity. The wretched Astraea, who is the perfection of beauty and innocence, has long been thus condemned for life. The romantic tales of virgins devoted to the jaws of monsters, have nothing in them so terrible as the gift of Astraea to that Bacchanal.

XXII.—NIGHT AND DAY.

From my own Apartment, December 13.

An old friend of mine being lately come to town, I went to see him on Tuesday last about eight o'clock in the evening, with a design to sit with him an hour or two and talk over old stories; but, upon inquiring after him, his servant told me he was just gone to bed. The next morning, as soon as I was up and dressed, and had despatched a little business, I came again to my friend's house about eleven o'clock, with a design to renew my visit: but, upon asking for him, his servant told me he was just sat down to dinner. In short, I found that my old-fashioned friend religiously adhered to the example of his forefathers, and observed the same hours that had been kept in the family ever since the Conquest.

It is very plain that the night was much longer formerly in this island than it is at present. By the night, I mean that portion of time which Nature has thrown into darkness, and which the wisdom of mankind had formerly dedicated to rest and silence. This used to begin at eight o'clock in the evening, and conclude at six in the morning. The curfew, or eight o'clock bell, was the signal throughout the nation for putting out their candles and going to bed.

Our grandmothers, though they were wont to sit up the last in the family, were all of them fast asleep at the same hours that their daughters are busy at crimp and basset. Modern statesmen are concerting schemes, and engaged in the depth of politics, at the time when their forefathers were laid down quietly to rest and had nothing in their heads but dreams. As we have thus thrown business and pleasure into the hours of rest, and by that means made the natural night but half as long as it should be, we are forced to piece it out with a great part of the morning; so that near two-thirds of the nation lie fast asleep for several hours in broad day-light. This irregularity is grown so very fashionable at present, that there is scarcely a lady of quality in Great Britain that ever saw the sun rise. And, if the humour increases in proportion to what it has done of late years, it is not impossible but our children may hear the bell-man going about the streets at nine o'clock in the morning, and the watch making their rounds till eleven. This unaccountable disposition in mankind to continue awake in the night and sleep in sunshine, has made me inquire, whether the same change of inclination has happened to any other animals? For this reason, I desired a friend of mine in the country to let me know whether the lark rises as early as he did formerly; and whether the cock begins to crow at his usual hour? My friend has answered me, "that his poultry are as regular as ever, and that all the birds and the beasts of his neighbourhood keep the same hours that they have observed in the memory of man; and the same which in all probability they have kept for these five thousand years."

If you would see the innovations that have been made among us in this particular, you may only look into the hours of colleges, where they still dine at eleven, and sup at six, which were doubtless the hours of the whole nation at the time when those places were founded. But at present, the courts of justice are scarce opened in Westminster Hall at the time when William Rufus used to go to dinner in it. All business is driven forward. The landmarks of our fathers, if I may so call them, are removed, and planted farther up into the day; insomuch, that I am afraid our clergy will be obliged, if they expect full congregations, not to look any more upon ten o'clock in the morning as a canonical hour. In my own memory, the dinner has crept by degrees from twelve o'clock to three, and where it will fix nobody knows.

I have sometimes thought to draw up a memorial in the behalf of Supper against Dinner, setting forth, that the said Dinner has made several encroachments upon the said Supper, and entered very far upon his frontiers; that he has banished him out of several families, and in all has driven him from his headquarters, and forced him to make his retreat into the hours of midnight; and, in short, that he is now in danger of being entirely confounded and lost in a breakfast. Those who have read Lucian, and seen the complaints of the letter T against S, upon account of many injuries and usurpations of the same nature, will not, I believe, think such a memorial forced and unnatural. If dinner has been thus postponed, or, if you please, kept back from time to time, you may be sure that it has been in compliance with the other business of the day, and that supper has still observed a proportionable distance. There is a venerable proverb which we have all of us heard in our infancy, of "putting the children to bed, and laying the goose to the fire." This was one of the jocular sayings of our forefathers, but maybe properly used in the literal sense at present. Who would not wonder at this perverted relish of those who are reckoned the most polite part of mankind, that prefer sea-coals and candles to the sun, and exchange so many cheerful morning hours, for the pleasures of midnight revels and debauches? If a man was only to consult his health, he would choose to live his whole time, if possible, in daylight, and to retire out of the world into silence and sleep, while the raw damps and unwholesome vapours fly abroad, without a sun to disperse, moderate, or control them. For my own part, I value an hour in the morning as much as common libertines do an hour at midnight. When I find myself awakened into being, and perceive my life renewed within me, and at the same time see the whole face of nature recovered out of the dark uncomfortable state in which it lay for several hours, my heart overflows with such secret sentiments of joy and gratitude, as are a kind of implicit praise to the great Author of Nature. The mind, in these early seasons of the day, is so refreshed in all its faculties, and borne up with such new supplies of animal spirits, that she finds herself in a state of youth, especially when she is entertained with the breath of flowers, the melody of birds, the dews that hang upon the plants, and all those other sweets of nature that are peculiar to the morning.

It is impossible for a man to have this relish of being, this exquisite taste of life, who does not come into the world before it is in all its noise and hurry; who loses the rising of the sun, the still hours of the day, and, immediately upon his first getting up plunges himself into the ordinary cares or follies of the world.

I shall conclude this paper with Milton's inimitable description of Adam's awakening his Eve in Paradise, which indeed would have been a place as little delightful as a barren heath or desert to those who slept in it. The fondness of the posture in which Adam is represented, and the softness of his whisper, are passages in this divine poem that are above all commendation, and rather to be admired than praised.

> Now Morn, her rosy steps in the eastern clime,
> Advancing, sowed the earth with orient pearl,
> When Adam waked, so customed; for his sleep
> Was airy light from pure digestion bred,
> And temperate vapours bland; which the only sound
> Of leaves and fuming rills, Aurora's fan,
> Lightly dispersed, and the shrill matin song
> Of birds on every bough; so much the more
> His wonder was to find unwakened Eve,
> With tresses discomposed, and glowing cheek,
> As through unquiet rest. He on his side
> Leaning half-raised, with looks of cordial love,
> Hung over her enamoured, and beheld
> Beauty, which, whether waking or asleep,
> Shot forth peculiar graces. Then, with voice
> Mild as when Zephyrus on Flora breathes,
> Her hand soft touching, whispered thus: "Awake,
> My fairest, my espoused, my latest found,
> Heaven's last, best gift, my ever-new delight,
> Awake; the morning shines, and the fresh field
> Calls us; we lose the prime, to mark how spring
> Our tended plants, how blows the citron grove,
> What drops the myrrh, and what the balmy reed,
> How Nature paints her colours, how the bee
> Sits on the bloom extracting liquid sweet."
> Such whispering waked her, but with startled eye
> On Adam, whom embracing, thus she spake:
> "O soul! in whom my thoughts find all repose,
> My glory, my perfection, glad I see
> Thy face, and morn returned."
>
> *Par. Lost*, V.1.

XXIII.—TWO OLD LADIES.

From my own Apartment, December 20, 1710.

It would be a good appendix to "The Art of Living and Dying" if any one would write "The Art of growing Old," and teach men to resign their pretensions to the pleasures and gallantries of youth in proportion to the alteration they find in themselves by the approach of age and infirmities. The infirmities of this stage of life would be much fewer if we did not affect those which attend the more vigorous and active part of our days; but instead of studying to be wiser, or being contented with our present follies, the ambition of many of us is also to be the same sort of fools we formerly have been. I have often argued, as I am a professed lover of women, that our sex grows old with a much worse grace than the other does; and have ever been of opinion that there are more well-pleased old women than old men. I thought it a good reason for this, that the ambition of the fair sex being confined to advantageous marriages, or shining in the eyes of men, their parts were over sooner, and consequently the errors in the performance of them. The conversation of this evening has not convinced me of the contrary; for one or two fop-women shall not make a balance for the crowd of coxcombs among ourselves, diversified according to the different pursuits of pleasure and business.

Returning home this evening, a little before my usual hour, I scarce had seated myself in my easy-chair, stirred the fire, and stroked my cat, but I heard somebody come rumbling upstairs. I saw my door opened, and a human figure advancing towards me so fantastically put together that it was some minutes before I discovered it to be my old and intimate friend Sam Trusty. Immediately I rose up, and placed him in my own seat; a compliment I pay to few. The first thing he uttered was, "Isaac, fetch me a cup of your cherry brandy before you offer to ask any question." He drank a lusty draught, sat silent for some time, and at last broke out: "I am come," quoth he, "to insult thee for an old fantastic dotard, as thou art, in ever defending the women. I have this evening visited two widows, who are now in that state I have often heard you call an after-life; I suppose you mean by it an existence which grows out of past entertainments, and is an untimely delight in the satisfactions which they once set their hearts upon too much to be ever able to relinquish. Have but patience," continued he, "till I give you a succinct account of my ladies and of this night's adventure. They are much of an age, but very different in their characters. The one of them, with all the advances which years have made upon her, goes on in a certain romantic road of love and friendship, which she fell into in her teens; the other has transferred the amorous passions of her first years to the love of cronies, pets, and favourites, with which she is always surrounded; but the genius of each of them will best appear by the account of what happened to me at their houses. About five this afternoon, being tired with study, the weather inviting, and time lying a little upon my hands, I resolved, at the instigation of my evil genius, to visit them; their husbands having been our contemporaries. This I thought I could do without much trouble; for both live in the very next street. I went first to my lady Camomile; and the butler, who had lived long in the family, and seen me often in his master's time, ushered me very civilly into the parlour, and told me, though my lady had given strict orders to be denied, he was sure I might be admitted, and bid the black boy acquaint his lady that I was come to wait upon her. In the window lay two letters; one broken open, the other fresh sealed with a wafer; the first directed to the divine Cosmelia, the second to the charming Lucinda; but both, by the indented characters, appeared to have been writ by very unsteady hands. Such uncommon addresses increased my curiosity, and put me upon asking my old friend the butler if he knew who those persons were. 'Very well,' says he; 'this is from Mrs. Furbish to my lady, an old schoolfellow and great crony of her ladyship's: and this the answer.' I inquired in what county she lived. 'Oh, dear!' says he, 'but just by, in the neighbourhood. Why, she was here all this morning, and that letter came and was answered within these two hours. They have taken an odd fancy, you must know, to call one another hard names; but, for all that, they love one another hugely.' By this time the boy returned with his lady's humble service to me, desiring I would excuse her; for she could not possibly see me, nor anybody else, for it was opera-night."

"Methinks," says I, "such innocent folly as two old women's courtship to each other should rather make you merry than put you out of humour." "Peace, good Isaac," says he, "no interruption, I beseech you. I got soon to Mrs. Feeble's, she that was formerly Betty Frisk; you must needs remember her; Tom Feeble, of Brazen Nose, fell in love with her for her fine dancing. Well, Mrs. Ursula, without further ceremony, carries me directly up to her mistress's chamber, where I found her environed by four of the most mischievous animals than can ever infest a family; an old shock dog with one eye, a monkey chained to one side of the chimney, a great grey squirrel to the other, and a parrot waddling in the middle of the room. However, for awhile all was in a profound tranquillity. Upon the mantle-tree, for I am a pretty curious observer, stood a pot of lambative electuary, with a stick of liquorice, and near it a phial of rose-water, and powder of tutty. Upon the table lay a pipe filled with betony and colt's-foot, a roll of wax-candle, a silver spitting-pot, and a Seville orange. The lady was placed in a large wicker chair, and her feet wrapped up in flannel, supported by cushions; and in this attitude—would you believe it, Isaac?—was she reading a romance with spectacles on. The first compliments over, as she was industriously endeavouring to enter upon conversation, a violent fit of coughing seized her. This awakened Shock, and in a trice the whole room was in an uproar; for the dog barked, the squirrel squealed, the monkey chattered, the parrot screamed, and Ursula, to appease them, was more clamorous than all the rest. You, Isaac, who know how any harsh noise affects my head, may guess what I suffered from the hideous din of these discordant sounds. At length all was appeased, and quiet restored: a chair was drawn for me; where I was no sooner seated, but the parrot fixed his horny beak, as sharp as a pair of shears, in one of my heels, just above the shoe. I sprang from the place with an unusual agility, and so, being within the monkey's reach, he snatches off my new bob-wig, and throws it upon two apples that were roasting by a sullen sea-coal fire. I was nimble enough to save it from any further damage than singeing the fore-top. I put it on; and composing myself as well as I could, I drew my chair towards the other side of the chimney. The good lady, as soon as she had recovered breath, employed it in making a thousand apologies, and, with great eloquence, and a numerous train of words, lamented my misfortune. In the middle of her harangue, I felt something scratching near my knee, and feeling what it should be, found the squirrel had got into my coat-pocket. As I endeavoured to remove him from his burrow, he made his teeth meet through the fleshy part of my forefinger. This gave me an unexpressible pain. The Hungary water was immediately brought to bathe it, and goldbeater's skin applied to stop the blood. The lady renewed her excuses; but, being now out of all patience, I abruptly took my leave, and hobbling downstairs with heedless haste, I set my foot full in a pail of water, and down we came to the bottom together." Here my friend concluded his narrative, and, with a composed countenance, I began to make him compliments of condolence; but he started from his chair, and said, "Isaac, you may spare your speeches; I expect no reply. When I told you this, I knew you would laugh at me; but the next woman that makes me ridiculous shall be a young one."

XXIV.—MARIA CALLS IN SHIRE LANE.

From my own Apartment, November 7, 1709.

I was very much surprised this evening with a visit from one of the top Toasts of the town, who came privately in a chair, and bolted into my room, while I was reading a chapter of Agrippa upon the occult sciences; but, as she entered with all the air and bloom that nature ever bestowed on woman, I threw down the conjurer, and met the charmer. I had no sooner placed her at my right hand by the fire, but she opened to me the reason of her visit. "Mr. Bickerstaff," said the fine creature, "I have been your correspondent some time, though I never saw you before; I have written by the name of Maria. You have told me you were too far gone in life to think of love. Therefore, I am answered as to the passion I spoke of; and," continued she, smiling, "I will not stay till you grow young again, as you men never fail to do in your dotage, but am come to consult you about disposing of myself to another. My person you see; my fortune is very considerable; but I am at present under much perplexity how to act in a great conjuncture. I have two lovers, Crassus and Lorio; Crassus is prodigiously rich, but has no one distinguishing quality; though at the same time he is not remarkable on the defective side. Lorio has travelled, is well bred, pleasant in discourse, discreet in his conduct, agreeable in his person; and, with all this, he has a competency of fortune without superfluity. When I consider Lorio, my mind is filled with an idea of the great satisfactions of a pleasant conversation. When I think of Crassus, my equipage, numerous servants, gay liveries, and various dresses, are opposed to the charms of his rival. In a word when I cast my eyes upon Lorio, I forget and despise fortune; when I behold Crassus, I think only of pleasing my vanity, and enjoying an uncontrolled expense in all the pleasures of life, except love." She paused here.

"Madam," said I, "I am confident that you have not stated your case with sincerity, and that there is some secret pang which you have concealed from me; for I see by your aspect the generosity of your mind; and that open, ingenuous air lets me know that you have too great a sense of the generous passion of love to prefer the ostentation of life in the arms of Crassus to the entertainments and conveniences of it in the company of your beloved Lorio: for so he is indeed, madam; you speak his name with a different accent from the rest of your discourse. The idea his image raises in you gives new life to your features, and new grace to your speech. Nay, blush not, madam; there is no dishonour in loving a man of merit. I assure you, I am grieved at this dallying with yourself, when you put another in competition with him, for no other reason but superior wealth."—"To tell you, then," said she, "the bottom of my heart, there is Clotilda lies by, and plants herself in the way of Crassus, and I am confident will snap him if I refuse him. I cannot bear to think that she will shine above me. When our coaches meet, to see her chariot hung behind with four footmen, and mine with but two: hers, powdered, gay, and saucy, kept only for show; mine, a couple of careful rogues that are good for something: I own I cannot bear that Clotilda should be in all the pride and wantonness of wealth, and I only in the ease and affluence of it."

Here I interrupted: "Well, madam, now I see your whole affliction; you could be happy, but that you fear another would be happier. Or rather, you could be solidly happy, but that another is to be happy in appearance. This is an evil which you must get over, or never know happiness. We will put the case, madam, that you married Crassus, and she Lorio." She answered: "Speak not of it; I could tear her eyes out at the mention of it."—"Well, then, I pronounce Lorio to be the man; but I must tell you that what we call settling in the world is, in a kind, leaving it; and you must at once resolve to keep your thoughts of happiness within the reach of your fortune, and not measure it by comparison with others."

XXV.—SISTER JENNY AND HER HUSBAND.

From my own Apartment, October
24.

My brother Tranquillus, who is a man of business, came to me this morning into my study, and after very many civil expressions in return for what good offices I had done him, told me "he desired to carry his wife, my sister, that very morning to his own house." I readily told him "I would wait upon him" without asking why he was so impatient to rob us of his good company. He went out of my chamber, and I thought seemed to have a little heaviness upon him, which gave me some disquiet. Soon after my sister came to me with a very matron-like air, and most sedate satisfaction in her looks, which spoke her very much at ease; but the traces of her countenance seemed to discover that she had lately been in a passion, and that air of content to flow from a certain triumph upon some advantage obtained. She no sooner sat down by me but I perceived she was one of those ladies who begin to be managers within the time of their being brides. Without letting her speak, which I saw she had a mighty inclination to do, I said, "Here has been your husband, who tells me he has a mind to go home this very morning, and I have consented to it."—- "It is well," said she, "for you must know—" "Nay, Jenny," said I, "I beg your pardon, for it is you must know. You are to understand, that now is the time to fix or alienate your husband's heart for ever; and I fear you have been a little indiscreet in your expressions or behaviour towards him, even here in my house." "There has," says she, "been some words; but I will be judged by you if he was not in the wrong: nay, I need not be judged by anybody, for he gave it up himself, and said not a word when he saw me grow passionate but, 'Madam, you are perfectly in the right of it:' as you shall judge—" " Nay, madam," said I, "I am judge already, and tell you that you are perfectly in the wrong of it; for if it was a matter of importance, I know he has better sense than you; if a trifle, you know what I told you on your wedding day, that you were to be above little provocations." She knows very well I can be sour upon occasion, therefore gave me leave to go on.

"Sister," said I, "I will not enter into the dispute between you, which I find his prudence put an end to before it came to extremity; but charge you to have a care of the first quarrel, as you tender your happiness; for then it is that the mind will reflect harshly upon every circumstance that has ever passed between you. If such an accident is ever to happen, which I hope never will, be sure to keep the circumstance before you; make no allusions to what is passed, or conclusions referring to what is to come; do not show a hoard of matter for dissension in your breast; but, if it is necessary, lay before him the thing as you understand it, candidly, without being ashamed of acknowledging an error, or proud of being in the right. If a young couple be not careful in this point they will get into a habit of wrangling; and when to displease is thought of no consequence, to please is always of as little moment. There is a play, Jenny, I have formerly been at when I was a student; we got into a dark corner with a porringer of brandy, and threw raisins into it, then set it on fire. My chamber-fellow and I diverted ourselves with the sport of venturing our fingers for the raisins; and the wantonness of the thing was to see each other look like a demon, as we burnt ourselves, and snatched out the fruit. This fantastical mirth was called Snap-Dragon. You may go into many a family, where you see the man and wife at this sport: every word at their table alludes to some passage between themselves; and you see by the paleness and emotion in their countenances that it is for your sake and not their own that they forbear playing out the whole game in burning each other's fingers. In this case, the whole purpose of life is inverted, and the ambition turns upon a certain contention, who shall contradict best, and not upon an inclination to excel in kindnesses and good offices. Therefore, dear Jenny, remember me, and avoid Snap-Dragon."

"I thank you, brother," said she, "but you do not know how he loves me; I find I can do anything with him."—"If you can so, why should you desire to do anything but please him? But I have a word or two more before you go out of the room; for I see you do not like the subject I am upon: let nothing provoke you to fall upon an imperfection he cannot help; for, if he has a resenting spirit, he will think your aversion as immovable as the imperfection with which you upbraid him. But above all, dear Jenny, be careful of one thing, and you will be something more than woman; that is, a levity you are almost all guilty of, which is, to take a pleasure in your power to give pain. It is even in a mistress an argument of meanness of spirit, but in a wife it is injustice and ingratitude. When a sensible man once observes this in a woman, he must have a very great, or very little, spirit to overlook it. A woman ought, therefore, to consider very often how few men there are who will regard a meditated offence as a weakness of temper."

I was going on in my confabulation, when Tranquillus entered. She cast all her eyes upon him with much shame and confusion, mixed with great complacency and love, and went up to him. He took her in his arms, and looked so many soft things at one glance that I could see he was glad I had been talking to her, sorry she had been troubled, and angry at himself that he could not disguise the concern he was in an hour before. After which he says to me, with an air awkward enough, but methought not unbecoming, "I have altered my mind, brother; we will live upon you a day or two longer." I replied, "That is what I have been persuading Jenny to ask of you, but she is resolved never to contradict your inclination, and refused me."

We were going on in that way which one hardly knows how to express; as when two people mean the same thing in a nice case, but come at it by talking as distantly from it as they can; when very opportunely came in upon us an honest, inconsiderable fellow, Tim Dapper, a gentleman well known to us both. Tim is one of those who are very necessary, by being very inconsiderable. Tim dropped in at an incident when we knew not how to fall into either a grave or a merry way. My sister took this occasion to make off, and Dapper gave us an account of all the company he had been in to-day, who was, and who was not at home, where he visited. This Tim is the head of a species: he is a little out of his element in this town; but he is a relation of Tranquillus, and his neighbour in the country, which is the true place of residence for this species. The habit of a Dapper, when he is at home, is a light broad-cloth, with calamanco or red waistcoat and breeches; and it is remarkable that their wigs seldom hide the collar of their coats. They have always a peculiar spring in their arms, a wriggle in their bodies, and a trip in their gait. All which motions they express at once in their drinking, bowing or saluting ladies; for a distant imitation of a forward fop, and a resolution to overtop him in his way, are the distinguishing marks of a Dapper. These under-characters of men are parts of the sociable world by no means to be neglected: they are like pegs in a building; they make no figure in it, but hold the structure together, and are as absolutely necessary as the pillars and columns. I am sure we found it so this morning; for Tranquillus and I should, perhaps, have looked cold at each other the whole day, but Dapper fell in, with his brisk way, shook us both by the hand, rallied the bride, mistook the acceptance he met with amongst us for extraordinary perfection in himself, and heartily pleased, and was pleased, all the while he stayed. His company left us all in good humour, and we were not such fools as to let it sink before we confirmed it by great cheerfulness and openness in our carriage the whole evening.

XVII.—LOVE THAT WILL LIVE.

From my own Apartment, December 7.

My brother Tranquillus being gone out of town for some days, my sister Jenny sent me word she would come and dine with me, and therefore desired me to have no other company. I took care accordingly, and was not a little pleased to see her enter the room with a decent and matron-like behaviour, which I thought very much became her. I saw she had a great deal to say to me, and easily discovered in her eyes, and the air of her countenance, that she had abundance of satisfaction in her heart, which she longed to communicate. However, I was resolved to let her break into her discourse her own way, and reduced her to a thousand little devices and intimations to bring me to the mention of her husband. But, finding I was resolved not to name him, she began of her own accord. "My husband," said she, "gives his humble service to you;" to which I only answered, "I hope he is well;" and, without waiting for a reply, fell into other subjects. She at last was out of all patience, and said, with a smile and manner that I thought had more beauty and spirit than I had ever observed before in her, "I did not think, brother, you had been so ill-natured. You have seen, ever since I came in, that I had a mind to talk of my husband, and you will not be so kind as to give me an occasion."—"I did not know," said I, "but it might be a disagreeable subject to you. You do not take me for so old-fashioned a fellow as to think of entertaining a young lady with the discourse of her husband. I know nothing is more acceptable than to speak of one who is to be so; but to speak of one who is so! indeed, Jenny, I am a better bred man than you think me." She showed a little dislike at my raillery, and by her bridling up, I perceived she expected to be treated hereafter not as Jenny Distaff, but Mrs. Tranquillus. I was very well pleased with this change in her humour; and, upon talking with her on several subjects, I could not but fancy that I saw a great deal of her husband's way and manner in her remarks, her phrases, the tone of her voice, and the very air of her countenance. This gave me an unspeakable satisfaction, not only because I had found her a husband from whom she could learn many things that were laudable, but also because I looked upon her imitation of him as an infallible sign that she entirely loved him. This is an observation that I never knew fail, though I do not remember that any other has made it. The natural shyness of her sex hindered her from telling me the greatness of her own passion; but I easily collected it from the representation she gave me of his. "I have everything," says she, "in Tranquillus that I can wish for; and enjoy in him, what indeed you have told me were to be met with in a good husband, the fondness of a lover, the tenderness of a parent, and the intimacy of a friend." It transported me to see her eyes swimming in tears of affection when she spoke. "And is there not, dear sister," said I, "more pleasure in the possession of such a man than in all the little impertinences of balls, assemblies, and equipage, which it cost me so much pains to make you contemn?" She answered, smiling, "Tranquillus has made me a sincere convert in a few weeks, though I am afraid you could not have done it in your whole life. To tell you truly, I have only one fear hanging upon me, which is apt to give me trouble in the midst of all my satisfactions: I am afraid, you must know, that I shall not always make the same amiable appearance in his eye that I do at present. You know, brother Bickerstaff,

86

that you have the reputation of a conjurer; and if you have any one secret in your art to make your sister always beautiful, I should be happier than if I were mistress of all the worlds you have shown me in a starry night." "Jenny," said I, "without having recourse to magic, I shall give you one plain rule that will not fail of making you always amiable to a man who has so great a passion for you, and is of so equal and reasonable a temper, as Tranquillus. Endeavour to please, and you must please; be always in the same disposition as you are when you ask for this secret, and you may take my word you will never want it. An inviolable fidelity, good-humour, and complacency of temper outlive all the charms of a fine face, and make the decays of it invisible."

We discoursed very long upon this head, which was equally agreeable to us both; for I must confess, as I tenderly love her, I take as much pleasure in giving her instructions for her welfare as she herself does in receiving them. I proceeded, therefore, to inculcate these sentiments by relating a very particular passage that happened within my own knowledge.

There were several of us making merry at a friend's house in a country village, when the sexton of the parish church entered the room in a sort of surprise, and told us "that, as he was digging a grave in the chancel, a little blow of his pick-axe opened a decayed coffin, in which there were several written papers." Our curiosity was immediately raised, so that we went to the place where the sexton had been at work, and found a great concourse of people about the grave. Among the rest there was an old woman, who told us the person buried there was a lady whose name I did not think fit to mention, though there is nothing in the story but what tends very much to her honour. This lady lived several years an exemplary pattern of conjugal love, and, dying soon after her husband, who every way answered her character in virtue and affection, made it her death-bed request, "that all the letters which she had received from him both before and after her marriage should be buried in the coffin with her." These I found, upon examination, were the papers before us. Several of them had suffered so much by time that I could only pick out a few words; as my soul! lilies! roses! dearest angel! and the like. One of them, which was legible throughout, ran thus:

"*Madam,*
  "If you would know the greatness of my love, consider that of your own beauty. That blooming countenance, that snowy bosom, that graceful person return every moment to my imagination; the brightness of your eyes hath hindered me from closing mine since I last saw you. You may still add to your beauties by a smile. A frown will make me the most wretched of men, as I am the most passionate of lovers."

It filled the whole company with a deep melancholy to compare the description of the letter with the person that occasioned it, who was now reduced to a few crumbling bones and a little mouldering heap of earth. With much ado I deciphered another letter, which began with, "My dear, dear wife." This gave me a curiosity to see how the style of one written in marriage differed from one written in courtship.

To my surprise, I found the fondness rather augmented than lessened, though the panegyric turned upon a different accomplishment. The words were as follows:

"Before this short absence from you, I did not know that I loved you so much as I really do; though, at the same time, I thought I loved you as much as possible. I am under great apprehensions lest you should have any uneasiness whilst I am defrauded of my share in it, and cannot think of tasting any pleasures that you do not partake with me. Pray, my dear, be careful of your health, if for no other reason but because you know I could not outlive you. It is natural in absence to make professions of an inviolable constancy; but towards so much merit it is scarce a virtue, especially when it is but a bare return to that of which you have given me such continued proofs ever since our first acquaintance. I am," *etc.*

It happened that the daughter of these two excellent persons was by when I was reading this letter. At the sight of the coffin, in which was the body of her mother near that of her father, she melted into a flood of tears. As I had heard a great character of her virtue, and observed in her this instance of filial piety, I could not resist my natural inclination of giving advice to young people, and therefore addressed myself to her. "Young lady," said I, "you see how short is the possession of that beauty in which nature has been so liberal to you. You find the melancholy sight before you is a contradiction to the first letter that you heard on that subject; whereas you may observe, the second letter, which celebrates your mother's constancy, is itself, being found in this place, an argument of it. But, madam, I ought to caution you not to think the bodies that lie before you your father and your mother. Know, their constancy is rewarded by a nobler union than by this mingling of their ashes, in a state where there is no danger or possibility of a second separation."

XXVI.—MR. BICKERSTAFF'S NEPHEWS.

From my own Apartment, June 16.

The vigilance, the anxiety, the tenderness, which I have for the good people of England, I am persuaded, will in time be much commended; but I doubt whether they will be ever rewarded. However, I must go on cheerfully in my work of reformation: that being my great design, I am studious to prevent my labours increasing upon me; therefore am particularly observant of the temper and inclinations of childhood and youth, that we may not give vice and folly supplies from the growing generation. It is hardly to be imagined how useful this study is, and what great evils or benefits arise from putting us in our tender years to what we are fit or unfit; therefore on Tuesday last, with a design to sound their inclinations, I took three lads, who are under my guardianship, a-rambling, in a hackney-coach, to show them the town; as the lions, the tombs, Bedlam, and the other places which are entertainments to raw minds because they strike forcibly on the fancy. The boys are brothers, one of sixteen, the other of fourteen, the other of twelve. The first was his father's darling, the second his mother's, and the third is mine, who am their uncle. Mr. William is a lad of true genius; but, being at the upper end of a great school, and having all the boys below him, his arrogance is insupportable. If I begin to show a little of my Latin, he immediately interrupts: "Uncle, under favour, that which you say is not understood in that manner." "Brother," says my boy Jack, "you do not show your manners much in contradicting my uncle Isaac!" "You queer cur," says Mr. William, "do you think my uncle takes any notice of such a dull rogue as you are?" Mr. William goes on, "He is the most stupid of all my mother's children; he knows nothing of his book; when he should mind that, he is hiding or hoarding his taws and marbles, or laying up farthings. His way of thinking is, four-and-twenty farthings make sixpence, and two sixpences a shilling; two shillings and sixpence half a crown, and two half crowns five shillings. So within these two months the close hunks has scraped up twenty shillings, and we will make him spend it all before he comes home." Jack immediately claps his hands into both pockets, and turns as pale as ashes. There is nothing touches a parent, and such I am to Jack, so nearly as a provident conduct. This lad has in him the true temper for a good husband, a kind father, and an honest executor. All the great people you see make considerable figures on the exchange, in court, and sometimes in senates, are such as in reality have no greater faculty than what may be called human instinct, which is a natural tendency to their own preservation, and that of their friends, without being capable of striking out of the road for adventures. There is Sir William Scrip was of this sort of capacity from his childhood; he has brought the country round him, and makes a bargain better than Sir Harry Wildfire, with all his wit and humour. Sir Harry never wants money but he comes to Scrip, laughs at him half an hour, and then gives bond for the other thousand. The close men are incapable of placing merit anywhere but in their pence, and therefore gain it; while others, who have larger capacities, are diverted from the pursuit by enjoyments which can be supported only by that cash which they despise; and therefore are in the end slaves to their inferiors both in fortune and understanding. I once heard a man of excellent sense observe, that more affairs in the world failed by being in the hands of men of too large capacities for their business, than by being in the conduct of such as wanted abilities to execute them. Jack, therefore, being of a plodding make, shall be a citizen: and I design him to be the refuge of the family in their distress, as well as their jest in prosperity. His brother Will shall go to Oxford with all speed, where, if he does not arrive at being a man of sense, he will soon be informed wherein he is a coxcomb. There is in that place such a true spirit of raillery and humour, that if they cannot make you a wise man, they will certainly let you know you are a fool; which is all my cousin wants, to cease to be so. Thus having taken these two out of the way, I have leisure to look at my third lad. I observe in the young rogue a natural subtlety of mind, which discovers itself rather in forbearing to declare his thoughts on any occasion, than in any visible way of exerting himself in discourse. For which reason I will place him where, if he commits no faults, he may go further than those in other stations, though they excel in virtues. The boy is well fashioned, and will easily fall into a graceful manner; wherefore I have a design to make him a page to a great lady of my acquaintance; by which means he will be well skilled in the common modes of life, and make a greater progress in the world by that knowledge than with the greatest qualities without it. A good mien in a court will carry a man greater lengths than a good understanding in any other place. We see a world of pains taken, and the best years of life spent in collecting a set of thoughts in a college for the conduct of life, and, after all the man so qualified shall hesitate in his speech to a good suit of clothes, and want common sense before an agreeable woman. Hence it is that wisdom, valour, justice, and learning cannot keep a man in countenance that is possessed of these excellences, if he wants that inferior art of life and behaviour called good breeding. A man endowed with great perfections, without this, is like one who has his pockets full of gold but always wants change for his ordinary occasions.

Will Courtly is a living instance of this truth, and has had the same education which I am giving my nephew. He never spoke a thing but what was said before, and yet can converse with the wittiest men without being ridiculous. Among the learned, he does not appear ignorant; nor with the wise, indiscreet. Living in conversation from his infancy makes him nowhere at a loss; and a long familiarity with the persons of men is, in a manner, of the same service to him as if he knew their arts. As ceremony is the invention of wise men to keep fools at a distance, so good breeding is an expedient to make fools and wise men equals.

My three nephews, whom, in June last twelve-month, I disposed of according to their several capacities and inclinations; the first to the university, the second to a merchant, and the third to a woman of quality as her page, by my invitation dined with me to-day. It is my custom often, when I have a mind to give myself a more than ordinary cheerfulness, to invite a certain young gentlewoman of our neighbourhood to make one of the company. She did me that favour this day. The presence of a beautiful woman of honour, to minds which are not trivially disposed, displays an alacrity which is not to be communicated by any other object. It was not unpleasant to me, to look into her thoughts of the company she was in. She smiled at the party of pleasure I had thought of for her, which was composed of an old man and three boys. My scholar, my citizen, and myself, were very soon neglected; and the young courtier, by the bow he made to her at her entrance, engaged her observation without a rival. I observed the Oxonian not a little discomposed at this preference, while the trader kept his eye upon his uncle. My nephew Will had a thousand secret resolutions to break in upon the discourse of his younger brother, who gave my fair companion a full account of the fashion, and what was reckoned most becoming to this complexion, and what sort of habit appeared best upon the other shape. He proceeded to acquaint her, who of quality was well or sick within the bills of mortality, and named very familiarly all his lady's acquaintance, not forgetting her very words when he spoke of their characters. Besides all this he had a load of flattery; and upon her inquiring what sort of woman Lady Lovely was in her person, "Really, madam," says the jackanapes, "she is exactly of your height and shape; but as you are fair, she is a brown woman." There was no enduring that this fop should outshine us all at this unmerciful rate; therefore I thought fit to talk to my young scholar concerning his studies; and, because I would throw his learning into present service, I desired him to repeat to me the translation he had made of some tender verses in Theocritus. He did so, with an air of elegance peculiar to the college to which I sent him. I made some exceptions to the turn of the phrases; which he defended with much modesty, as believing in that place the matter was rather to consult the softness of a swain's passion than the strength of his expressions. It soon appeared that Will had outstripped his brother in the opinion of our young lady. A little poetry, to one who is bred a scholar, has the same effect that a good carriage of his person has on one who is to live in courts. The favour of women is so natural a passion, that I envied both the boys their success in the approbation of my guest; and I thought the only person invulnerable was my young trader. During the whole meal, I could observe in the children a mutual contempt and scorn of each other, arising from their different way of life and education, and took that occasion to advertise them of such growing distastes, which might mislead them in their future life, and disappoint their friends, as well as themselves, of the advantages which might be expected from the diversity of their professions and interests.

The prejudices which are growing up between these brothers from the different ways of education are what create the most fatal misunderstandings in life. But all distinctions of disparagement, merely from our circumstances, are such as will not bear the examination of reason. The courtier, the trader, and the scholar, should all have an equal pretension to the denomination of a gentleman. That tradesman who deals with me in a commodity which I do not understand, with uprightness, has much more right to that character than the courtier who gives me false hopes, or the scholar who laughs at my ignorance.

The appellation of gentleman is never to be affixed to a man's circumstances, but to his behaviour in them. For this reason I shall ever, as far as I am able, give my nephews such impressions as shall make them value themselves rather as they are useful to others, than as they are conscious of merit in themselves. There are no qualities for which we ought to pretend to the esteem of others but such as render us serviceable to them: for "free men have no superiors but benefactors."

Printed in Great Britain
by Amazon

31641809R00056